COMP ASSISTED LEGAL RESEARCH

THE BASICS

By

Penny A. Hazelton
Law Librarian and Professor of Law
University of Washington

AMERICAN CASEBOOK SERIES®

WEST PUBLISHING CO.
ST. PAUL, MINN., 1993

COPYRIGHT © 1993 By WEST PUBLISHING CO.
610 Opperman Drive
P.O. Box 64526
St. Paul, MN 55164–0526
1–800–328–9352

All rights reserved
Printed in the United States of America

Library of Congress Cataloging-in-Publication Data
Hazelton, Penny A.
  Computer assisted legal research : the basics / by Penny Hazelton.
    p.   cm.
  ISBN 0–314–02266–X
  1. Legal research—United States—Data processing. 2. Information storage and retrieval systems—Law—United States. I. Title.
KF242.A1H49 1993
340′.0285—dc20   93–15371
                                                                 CIP

ISBN 0–314–02266–X

Hazelton, Comp.Research
1st Reprint—1995

To Norris and Tori
For Your Patience and Support

*

Preface

I have been teaching legal research since 1976 and computer-assisted legal research (CALR) since 1986. In preparation for a program aimed at educating attorneys about the power and flexibility of computer-assisted legal research in 1985, the reference librarians working with me and I became frustrated with the lack of good introductory materials. After reviewing the existing vendor-published material as well as the legal research texts available at the time, we decided we would need to write our own material for this continuing legal education program.

The CLE program which we started has been offered at least once a year since 1986, often twice a year. The purpose of the materials we prepared to accompany the 7 hour program was to help those with little exposure to CALR understand how the computer systems actually worked. The seminar was not a training session, but rather a program emphasizing the theoretical and practical consequences of searching full-text databases using computers. In addition, lest the unwary assume that computers answered all legal research questions equally well, we began analyzing the strengths and weaknesses of computer and manual (traditional) research.

This text is written for the same purpose. Revised and updated from Chapter 9 of Professor Marjorie Rombauer's 5th Edition of *Legal Problem Solving* (1991), this publication attempts to cover the basic concepts needed for the law student, paralegal or lawyer to understand when and how to capture the power and flexibility of CALR. I have been assigning this reading to my legal research students (law and library science students) since 1989 before the students attend their required hands-on training session. These materials have also been used in the first year Basic Legal Skills class and the Legal Methods class here at the University of Washington. I teach research only, so I do not use Professor Rombauer's entire text in my classes. Separate publication of the CALR chapter of her book meets the needs of those who teach research courses without a writing component.

The reading materials can be assigned separately, depending on the order in which the instructor is handling the teaching of CALR. At the University of Washington we teach the section on "Essential Searches Using Citations" before we train the students to use WESTLAW and LEXIS for other purposes.

This publication serves two other important purposes. First, the inclusion of the section on "Integrating Manual and Computer Research" helps the students realize that computers cannot always do everything better than traditional, printed tools. Since CALR is often taught in an isolated way, the student is at least exposed to the notion that the best legal research will be done by those who understand the strengths and weaknesses of computer-assisted legal research systems.

Secondly, "An Illustration of Applied Research Strategies" permits the student to see how to integrate the use of books and computer research to solve problems. By using the framework devised by Professor Rombauer and followed in her text, *Legal Problem Solving*, the student researches a problem which includes suggestions about where in the process computer resources might be used most effectively.

I am indebted to Melissa Landers and Kelly Kunsch who worked with me on that first CLE in 1986. They both helped me think through what it was that attorneys would need to know about the emerging CALR systems, short of a training session. I would also like to thank Professor Marjorie Rombauer for asking me in 1989 to revise the CALR chapter in the new edition of her book. This gave me the chance to refine and rethink the CLE materials. And, most importantly, I was delighted to work with Marjorie, a wonderful person as well as a superb writer. To Scott Burson, the author of the chapter on CALR in the 4th edition of *Legal Problem Solving*, thanks for providing the overarching framework and several passages which have been left intact.

I owe a debt of gratitude to librarians, students and library users who helped me formulate the questions that needed to be answered in this text. And, finally, thanks to Janet Abbott, a wonderful secretary and person, who typed and word-processed most of the pieces of this publication over and over and over again!

Penny A. Hazelton

Seattle 1993

Introduction

This booklet is designed to be read before you have a hands-on training session on any computer-assisted legal research (CALR) system. The information contained herein will not replicate what you will learn when you have a real terminal in front of you, but instead endeavors to help you understand how the computer reads and processes the messages, or searches, you send it. There is less emphasis on how to perform the desired function (a hands-on training session is best for this) and more emphasis on why certain functions should be performed and why certain results are achieved.

This overview of CALR could really be used to understand almost any electronic legal research system, including many of the CD–ROM products now being marketed. Because of the pervasive nature of WESTLAW and LEXIS, they provide the focus for this text.

The researcher needs to understand little about the operation of CALR systems in order to do the essential searches which can be performed simply by using citations. If more complex research must be done using the computer, understanding the basics of how computers process your query is important. Some general comments about using CALR are followed by an in-depth look at strategies needed to integrate traditional, print sources and computerized tools. Then, using the Rombauer research framework, research of a specific problem helps you grasp how the use of both manual and computer tools might actually work. Finally, CD–ROM technology is explored followed by a section on non-legal databases.

Completing the readings contained in this text should help you appreciate the complexities and power computer-assisted legal research systems have brought to the solution of legal problems.

*

Table of Contents

		Page
Preface		v
Introduction		vii

I.	INTRODUCTION: COMPUTER–ASSISTED LEGAL RESEARCH SYSTEMS	1
II.	ESSENTIAL SEARCHES USING CITATIONS	6
	A. General Observations	6
	B. Search for Document When Citation is Known	6
	C. Case Verification	8
III.	CALR SEARCH BASICS	18
	A. Overview	18
	B. Definition of a Word	19
	C. Noise Stop Words and Common Words	19
	D. Truncation	20
	E. Plurals	22
	F. Compound Words	23
	G. Synonyms	23
IV.	QUERY FORMULATION: TERMS AND CONNECTORS	25
	A. The *OR* Connector	25
	B. The *AND* Connector	26
	C. The *AND NOT* or *BUT NOT* Connector	27
	D. Multiple Connectors	28
	E. Proximity Connectors	29
	F. Summary of Connectors	30
	G. Order of Processing	31
	H. Organization of Documents in the Databases	33
V.	QUERY FORMULATION: NATURAL LANGUAGE SEARCHING	39
	A. Overview	39
	B. Strengths	39
	C. Limitations	40
	D. Conclusions	41
VI.	CONDUCTING RESEARCH ON CALR SYSTEMS	42
	A. General Observations	42
	B. Going Online	42
	C. Summary	45
VII.	INTEGRATING MANUAL AND COMPUTER RESEARCH	47
	A. The Nature of Legal Research Tools	47
	B. Variables That Will Affect Selection of Research Tools	50
	C. Manual Research Tools Are Better When	52

TABLE OF CONTENTS

Page

VII. INTEGRATING MANUAL AND COMPUTER RESEARCH—Continued
- D. Computerized Research Tools Are Better When 56
- E. Summary 61

VIII. AN ILLUSTRATION OF APPLIED RESEARCH STRATEGIES 62
- A. Refresher 62
- B. Preliminary Analysis 63
- C. Search for Statutes 64
- D. Search for Mandatory Case Authority 66
- E. Search for Persuasive Case Authority 67
- F. Refine Issues and Analysis: Doublecheck & Verify Case and Statutory Authority 67
- G. Summary 68

IX. MORE ABOUT NEW TECHNOLOGY: CD–ROM 69
- A. In General 69
- B. Characteristics of CD–ROM Products 69
- C. The Legal CD–ROM Market Today 70

X. NON–LEGAL DATABASES 72
- A. Nexis 72
- B. Dialog 72
- C. Others 73

COMPUTER ASSISTED LEGAL RESEARCH
THE BASICS

*

I. INTRODUCTION: COMPUTER-ASSISTED LEGAL RESEARCH SYSTEMS

Imagine a printed index to legal authorities that would allow users to locate any word used in any authority. An index that would be compiled instantaneously upon receipt of material, so that there would be no delay between the time material is available and the time material is readily accessible. An index infinitely specific and infinitely flexible that included entries for any combination of two or more words. Imagine the value to a legal researcher of being able to create an ad hoc index of all relevant primary material tailored specifically to the research problem at hand.

But imagine the nightmare of using such an index: It would require thousands of printed volumes to list the location of every word in relation to every other word occurring in even a relatively small number of reported decisions; new material would have to be added daily; updating material could rarely be cumulative by virtue of sheer bulk and frequency. It would take hours to use such a printed index.

Nevertheless, something approaching such an index is available today. The index is not printed; it is compiled, published, and made accessible electronically, using computers, computer terminals, and telecommunications equipment. It does not index every opinion. It does not index every word in the opinions that it does index. It is not quite infinitely flexible. It is not quite infinitely specific. But compared to printed research materials, it represents a new generation of tools available to the legal researcher. "It" is conventionally referred to as a computer-assisted legal research (CALR) system. In fact, there are two such indexes, or systems, commercially available.[1] One system, called LEXIS, is a service provided by Mead Data Central. The other system, called WESTLAW, is a service of West Publishing Company. These systems are capable of tremendous flexibility, specificity, and speed.

These two systems have been referred to by James Sprowl, one of the early students of CALR, as "generic retrieval mechanisms."[2] Sprowl uses the term generic not in the sense of being slightly off-

---

1. Though emphasis in this text is on the two most common online systems available in law schools (and the commercial sector), many of the general principles of search basics are applicable to any legal research system whose text is in electronic form. CD–ROM products, for example, are discussed briefly in section IX, but they have many of the same search characteristics of online legal databases.

2. Sprowl, *Legal Research and the Computer: Where the Two Paths Cross*, 15 Clearinghouse Rev. 150 (1981).

quality and low-priced, but in the sense of being readily adaptable to particular research problems on an ad hoc basis. As Sprowl points out, conventionally printed indexes point the researcher toward particular access points and entry terms. In this sense, they are not as adaptable on an ad hoc basis as computerized systems. Although the existing printed search tools of American law are generally excellent—perhaps the envy of all other disciplines of human intellectual endeavor in terms of their scope, coordination, specificity, and ease of use—nevertheless, these printed tools are often not adequately flexible; they sometimes lack specificity; occasionally they incompletely or erroneously analyze issues; they are not instantaneously available. CALR systems overcome many of these shortcomings and therefore have become important additional tools available to the legal researcher.

CALR systems are accessible with a computer terminal, keyboard, modem, communications software, and a telephone line or access to the Internet.[3] Since the early 1980s both WESTLAW and LEXIS have been working on compatibility with the world of personal computers, in addition to offering their dedicated terminals[4] for lease and/or sale. Now LEXIS and WESTLAW can be accessed with either company's "smart" personal computer workstation or with almost any computer terminal and modem manufactured. Both companies have written communications software that makes the sign-on procedure very easy, though off-the-shelf communications software packages such as Pro-Comm and Cross–Talk can also be used.

Most law schools now provide a variety of equipment for CALR use. Dedicated terminals are still common, though the use of personal computers in a special lab setting is growing. A mix of equipment will also be found in the private firm sector, again with growing emphasis on personal computers.

WESTLAW and LEXIS are dynamic and powerful systems, responsive to the legal marketplace. The companies are constantly changing

---

3. Increasingly, law schools are using the Internet instead of commercial phone lines to access WESTLAW and LEXIS. Both vendors have written communications software that permits their remote databases to be accessed by your computer terminal using the Internet. The Internet is a world-wide network of many individual networks (at least two computers linked together) which inter-connects the computers of the academic, government and private sectors. Not only does the Internet give access to the resources of other Internet computer networks, but it also permits communication directly with millions of other Internet users (electronic mail, real time discussion groups).

4. Dedicated terminals were first developed by LEXIS (Deluxe terminal) and later by WESTLAW (WALT terminal). They were designed with special keyboards to make use of the system as easy and straightforward as possible. Not only are the keyboards designed to activate commonly used procedures directly at a single touch, but the hardware is very easy to install. A dedicated terminal simply needs an outlet and a telephone line. The modem (the piece of hardware that allows access to a telephone line) is internal and so is the special communications software that makes the sign-on procedure so easy. The dedicated terminals are dumb; that is, they cannot perform other functions such as run word processing, spread sheet, or database management programs. The new generation of dedicated terminals, UBIQ II (LEXIS) and the WALT II (WESTLAW), are still not smart but they do permit the user to access other online databases through gateways.

the systems—adding new databases and enhancing old ones, refining software to make the systems more flexible and powerful. Because of the constant changes, this chapter is not a "how-to manual." Instead, it is intended to introduce the reader to current CALR systems in the hope that the reader will develop a sense of the potential of these systems: what they are, how they work, and when they should be used.

This text cannot, and does not attempt to, provide complete, detailed instruction on the mechanics of operation of either system. For specific information about the operation of LEXIS, WESTLAW, or any other CALR system, consult the literature published by and available from the vendor.[5]

Two texts written for the vendors by law librarians explore CALR systems in the context of legal research as a whole. These publications are actually a good guide to legal research generally, with a strong orientation to the use of CALR. Neither refers to their competitor system, limiting their usefulness as a general legal research text. However, both are well written and worth reading. Professor Kathy Carrick wrote *LEXIS: A Legal Research Manual* (Mead Data Central, 1989) and Professors Nancy Johnson, Bob Berring and Tom Woxland collaborated on *Winning Research Skills* (West, 1991).

Neither LEXIS nor WESTLAW in their training sessions give sufficient emphasis to the importance of reading the documentation associated with each system. This may reflect an assumption that attorneys will avoid a research tool that requires investment of time and energy to master. The result is that users are eased into the

---

5. WESTLAW and LEXIS both publish a variety of printed guides to system use. The most comprehensive of these are *Westlaw Reference Manual* (5th ed. 1993) and *Reference Manual for the LEXIS/NEXIS Services* (1991). More extensive database information can be found in the companion volumes, *LEXIS/NEXIS Product Guides* v. 1–6 (1993). Convenient desk reference cards are available from both vendors. These summarize available commands and connectors and remind users of the elements of search logic that may aid in constructing effective queries. WESTLAW also publishes a monthly newsletter highlighting new databases and enhancements to the systems. *WESTLAW Password* is a very helpful publication filled with news and tips about effective use of WESTLAW. Law schools normally receive multiple copies of *WESTLAW Password* for distribution to staff, faculty, and students. WESTLAW also prints and distributes a newsletter specifically for law schools entitled, *Class Actions*.

Early on both systems relied on their online menu and directory screens to provide lists of available files and databases. As the new databases added continued to grow at impossibly high rates, the vendors finally met a user need by publishing lists of their databases. Now both systems publish, at least twice a year, a directory of all online files. The *Westlaw Database List* and the *LEXIS/NEXIS Library Contents and Alphabetical List* both describe material loaded online and include the library or database name, the file name or database identifier, the material in the system, and the dates of coverage of the material online. In addition, both directories include a complete alphabetical list of all titles contained in the database so a user can, at a glance, find out whether the Washington Attorney General Opinions, for example, are on WESTLAW and LEXIS and if so, how far back the file extends. Additionally, both vendors are publishing exceptionally good training manuals. *Learning LEXIS: A Handbook for Modern Legal Research* (1992) and *Discovering WESTLAW: The Essential Guide* (3d ed. 1993) can be used as excellent introductions to CALR systems. *Discovering WESTLAW* has good problems throughout to test the reader's understanding and knowledge.

system without being fully aware of its capabilities. In commercial environments where online time results in client charges, this is inexcusable. If a researcher is unwilling to invest the time and effort to gain a complete understanding of CALR system operation, he or she should not attempt to use such systems. The cost associated with ignorance is too high.

Computer-assisted legal research systems operate by allowing a researcher at a computer terminal to perform searches of large databases of primary and secondary material stored in electronic format at a distant location. The cost of CALR use (for all but academic institutional subscribers) relates directly to the time the terminal is connected to the remote computer database (online time). Specific billing practices and costs differ between WESTLAW and LEXIS. On both systems, however, wasted time online translates directly into wasted money. Some institutional CALR subscribers (most notably law schools) pay for CALR use on a flat-rate subscription basis. Subscribers with this pricing policy can afford to be much more adventuresome and experimental in their CALR research since there is no danger of prohibitively high costs because of heavy online use. This text proceeds on the assumption (erroneous in the case of most law schools) that the student-researcher will pay ordinary commercial rates for his or her research. This approach is used to sensitize students to the environment in which most will ultimately make use of CALR systems.

Both WESTLAW and LEXIS allow users to conduct research in a variety of law related materials by using the storage and retrieval capability of large computers. The researcher, once signed onto the system, selects a database or file and then frames a search query using terms relevant to the issue being researched. The researcher types the search query on the keyboard of a terminal, and the computer directly searches the source documents in the specific database for the terms in the search query. Often CALR research saves time compared to conventional research because the computers operate with great speed.

The basic material (called source documents) that may be searched in both LEXIS and WESTLAW consists of databases of the texts of reported and unreported opinions of state and federal courts,[6] state and federal statutes, most federal and some state administrative and regulatory documents, many looseleaf services, legal periodical articles, some foreign law (primary sources), and many Shepard's Citators. Each system offers sources not available on the other, and the inclusive dates for materials offered in both often differ.

---

6. Full text searching on WESTLAW permits access to the editorial enhancements associated with the publications of West Publishing Company as well as to the full text of source documents; thus, it is possible to search headnotes, synopses, particular digest topics, key numbers, annotations, and historical references. LEXIS does not edit or enhance any of the documents it loads online, except in their creation of document segments. Segments and the WESTLAW equivalent, fields, will be described later in section IV.H.

Sec. I INTRODUCTION

Current database lists should be consulted for availability of specific material. Since both systems are constantly expanding the materials available for searching, the online directory should always be consulted as well since it will be more current than the printed directory. The WESTLAW online directory, with excellent descriptions and tips, can be consulted from within a database with the SCOPE command. The LEXIS online directory is consulted from the file menu by entering the page number shown for the file whose directory you want to see. The LEXIS directory is not as helpful or comprehensive as its WESTLAW equivalent.

II. ESSENTIAL SEARCHES USING CITATIONS

A. GENERAL OBSERVATIONS

Two uses of the CALR systems are essential in today's world of modern legal research. Furthermore, these two kinds of searching on LEXIS and WESTLAW require very little understanding of how the systems operate. The sign-on protocol will need to be learned, and since this varies with the type of terminal and software being used, the appropriate vendor manuals must be consulted. Once getting into the system is mastered, however, performing the mechanical searches is very easy.

The first type of essential search permits the researcher to quickly locate a copy of an entire document when the correct citation is known. Many times during the course of research, a citation is found for a case, statute, regulation, administration decision, law review article, or A.L.R. annotation that looks interesting. With access to WESTLAW and LEXIS, you can locate this document quickly and efficiently for review.

The second type of essential search that is done using a valid citation is case verification. The authority of cases can be checked online by Shepardizing, by using Shepard's PreView (WESTLAW only), by using LEXCITE (LEXIS) and Quick*Cite* (WESTLAW), by using the CALR systems as a citator, and by using Insta–Cite (WESTLAW) and Auto–Cite (LEXIS). Though Shepardizing (including Shepard's PreView) can be done in printed tools, the other five case verification techniques have no print equivalent. In addition, Shepard's PreView LEXCITE, Quick*Cite,* Insta–Cite, Auto–Cite and the system used as a citator, *are much more current than Shepard's.* Thus, these online services are essential tools, required in order for case verification to be absolutely current.

B. SEARCH FOR DOCUMENT WHEN CITATION IS KNOWN

Both WESTLAW and LEXIS permit the researcher to quickly locate a specific case, statute, or other kind of document in the databases. On WESTLAW the FIND command permits you to retrieve, for example, a specific case or statute for which you have a valid citation. Cases can be retrieved by docket number as well. The comparable LEXIS commands are LEXSEE and LEXSTAT. Though other kinds of searches could be done to locate these documents, these simple commands are faster and easier, and thus, more efficient.

FIND, LEXSEE, or LEXSTAT can be used to quickly retrieve an increasing number of types of documents beyond court opinions and statutes.[7] Both CALR systems provide online a list of the types of documents that can be located with these commands. Regardless of the type of research you are performing (manual or computer), a search that permits a researcher to quickly retrieve a known document will be of enormous assistance when the needed document (1) may never be published, (2) may be in the library's collection but missing from the shelf, (3) may not be physically located near the researcher, or (4) may not yet be published in any print form.

Searching for a document online when a citation is known lends itself nicely to the task of cite-checking legal documents. In addition, since almost all case opinions on WESTLAW and LEXIS are now star-paged to the actual print sources, most law reviews could do a great deal of their cite-checking without having to consult the books themselves. Obviously, this use of the computers will only work when the cites to be checked are cases and other documents which are actually loaded on WESTLAW and LEXIS and have been star paged to the original print source.

Once a document is found through FIND, LEXSEE, or LEXSTAT, the researcher may read or browse the document online, print it online or offline, or download the document text to a floppy or hard disk. The cost and availability of each of these options will probably dictate which one is selected.[8]

Another feature of LEXIS and WESTLAW needs to be mentioned here. JUMP (WESTLAW) and LINK (LEXIS) allow a searcher to jump immediately to another document cited within the text of a document being read on the screen. This hypertext enhancement means the

---

7. When first announced in the mid-1980s, the commands did not work for every type of document in the databases. Specifically, many administrative decisions, rulings, and reports could not be retrieved with these commands. For both LEXIS and WESTLAW, these commands are being expanded to cover most, if not all, of the documents in their vast databases.

8. Although a complete discussion of costs is outside the scope of this chapter, a note about browsing, reading and printing costs is in order. Reading documents online is not very cost effective. That is because WESTLAW and LEXIS charge for every minute you are connected to the database (online time). In addition, if every law student reads documents online, terminals would not be available for other students' use. Browsing documents may be very cost effective, however, especially if it reduces the number you would otherwise have to read in full in printed form or online.

Printing online may also not be cost effective. Online printing and downloading is done one page at a time. The CALR system charges for your online or connect time which, depending on the length of the document, may be quite time-consuming. Online printing is used primarily for printing lists and other short documents.

Offline printing or downloading (to a disk) permits the researcher to execute a print command, which tells the terminal to print the document all at one time either to paper or another computer. Both systems charge separately *by the line* for offline printing and downloading. Offline printing is usually available in law schools. But check to see what guidelines your law school uses for offline printing. If you cannot offline print, your only option is to print or download (if you are using a personal computer) online. Printing an entire document may be necessary if, for example, the document itself is not yet in printed form or its published source is not easily available to you. A recent enhancement on WESTLAW allows the printer to print a case document in dual columns so the resulting computer printout resembles the printed National Reporter volumes.

researcher does not have to use the LEXSEE, LEXSTAT or FIND commands discussed above once a document has been retrieved, thus saving several steps and precious time.

C. CASE VERIFICATION

Another type of research that can be performed on a CALR system when a citation is known is case verification.[9] This section will discuss case verification from the most comprehensive source to the most current sources. *In practice, the most current sources, Insta–Cite or Auto–Cite, should usually be checked first.* Both systems have loaded many units of the printed Shepard's Citators.[10] Shepardizing of cases can be performed online quickly and efficiently with the case citation. *However, the online files are no more current than the printed equivalent.* Nevertheless, online Shepardizing has advantages over manual Shepardizing.

Advantages include easier and speedier searches. In addition to cumulating the lists of citing cases online in one place (a substantial plus over use of the printed version), both LEXIS and WESTLAW write out the analysis or treatment (instead of using j, for example, the systems remind you that j means dissenting opinion), and permit you to retrieve the text of a citing case. Depending on the system you are using, the online Shepard's display may cite you to the first page of the opinion of the citing case as well as to the page on which your case is cited. Another significant feature permits the display of citing cases to be limited. For example, in Shepardizing a case you may discover that there are 60 pages of citing cases. If you are particularly interested only in seeing how often your case has been distinguished or cited in dissenting opinions, you can ask the computer to look through the 60 pages of citing cases and retrieve only those that meet your requirements. Similarly, WESTLAW can limit the display to citing cases published in a particular reporter and to citing cases from a specific court. Both WESTLAW and LEXIS can limit their displays to citing cases that refer to a particular headnote number. All these features make online Shepardizing very attractive. If given a choice between a search in the printed volumes and online, legal researchers should Shepardize cases online because of the flexibility of the online version. See Illustrations 1 and 2.

9. At the present time it is not possible to Insta–Cite or Auto–Cite statutory citations.

10. Check the online and printed directories for specific information as to which citators are available for searching. For example, both systems have added the state, federal and regional reporter Shepard's, but most of the online files do not go as far back as the printed product. The scope of Shepard's coverage online will be displayed each time you shepardize on WESTLAW and LEXIS.

ILLUSTRATION 1

Shepardizing Online

WESTLAW DISPLAY

Shepard's   PAGE 1

SHEPARD'S   (Rank 1 of 2)   Page 1 of 10

CITATIONS TO: 480 U.S. 202
CITATOR: UNITED STATES CITATIONS
DIVISION: United States Supreme Court Reports
COVERAGE: 1943–1988 Bound Supplement through Dec 1992 Supp; for more see SCOPE

Retrieval No.	---------Analysis---------	----------Citation----------	Headnote No.
		Same Text	(94 L.Ed.2d 244)	
1		Same Text	(107 S.Ct. 1083)	
2	SC	Same Case	783 F.2d 900	
	J	Dissenting Opin	490 U.S. at 209	
			57 U.S.L.W. at 4458	
			59 U.S.L.W. at 4139	
			60 U.S.L.W. at 4069	
			60 U.S.L.W. at 4072	
	J	Dissenting Opin	60 U.S.L.W. at 4074	
			90 U.S.L.W. at 4069	
			90 U.S.L.W. at 4072	
	J	Dissenting Opin	90 U.S.L.W. at 4074	
			U.S.Dk 90–408	

Note: Check Shepard's PreView (SP), Insta–Cite (IC), and QuickCite (QC). Copyright (C) 1993 McGraw-Hill, Inc.; Copyright (C) 1993 West Publishing Co.

SHEPARD'S   (Rank 1 of 2)   Page 2 of 10

CITATIONS TO: 480 U.S. 202
CITATOR: UNITED STATES CITATIONS
DIVISION: United States Supreme Court Reports

Retrieval No.	---------Analysis---------	------------Citation------------	Headnote No.
	J	Dissenting Opin	U.S.Dk 90–408	
			U.S.Dk 90–577	
	J	Dissenting Opin	U.S.Dk 90–577	
			Cir. DC	
1	E	Explained	850 F.2d 729, 737	2
2	E	Explained	663 F.Supp. 1300, 1310	
3			740 F.Supp. 9, 14	2
			Cir. 2	
4			845 F.2d 37, 40	1
5			913 F.2d 1024, 1025	2

        * * *

Copyright (C) 1993 McGraw–Hill, Inc.; Copyright (C) 1993 West Publishing Co.

ILLUSTRATION 2

Shepardizing Online

LEXIS DISPLAY

(c) 1993 McGraw–Hill, Inc. DOCUMENT 1 (OF 2)

CITATIONS TO: 480 U.S. 202
SERIES: SHEPARD'S UNITED STATES CITATIONS
DIVISION: UNITED STATES SUPREME COURT REPORTS
COVERAGE: Shepard's 1943–1986 Supplements Through 12/92 Supplement.

NUMBER	ANALYSIS	CITING REFERENCE	SYLLABUS/HEADNOTE
1	parallel citation	(94 L.Ed.2d 244)	
2	parallel citation	(107 S.Ct. 1083)	
3	same case	783 F.2d 900	
4	dissenting opinion	490 U.S. 209	
5		57 U.S.L.W. 4458	
6		59 U.S.L.W. 4139	
7		60 U.S.L.W. 4069	
8		60 U.S.L.W. 4072	
9	dissenting opinion	60 U.S.L.W. 4074	
—		90 U.S.L.W. 4069	
—		90 U.S.L.W. 4072	

(c) 1993 McGraw–Hill, Inc. DOCUMENT 1 (OF 2)
480 U.S. 202

NUMBER	ANALYSIS	CITING REFERENCE	SYLLABUS/HEADNOTE
—	dissenting opinion	90 U.S.L.W. 4074	
—		U.S.Dkt.No. 90–408	
—	dissenting opinion	U.S.Dkt.No. 90–408	
—		U.S.Dkt.No. 90–577	
—	dissenting opinion	U.S.Dkt.No. 90–577 Cir.D.C.	
17	explained	850 F.2d 737	2
18	explained	663 F.Supp. 1310	
19		740 F.Supp. 14 Cir. 2	2
20		845 F.2d 40	1
21		913 F.2d 1025	2
22	followed	913 F.2d 1029	1
23	distinguished	671 F.Supp. 222	2
24		725 F.Supp. 125	1

To see the text of a citing case, press the citing reference NUMBER and then the TRANSMIT key.
For further explanation, press the H key (for HELP) and then the TRANSMIT key.
Press Alt–H for Help or Alt–Q to Quit.

Because the Shepard's online product is no more current than the printed product, in 1989 **WESTLAW** announced an enhancement of Shepard's online, Shepard's PreView. A product of a joint venture between West and McGraw–Hill and currently only available on **WESTLAW**, Shepard's PreView provides the most current online citations to cases that appear in the advance sheets of the National Reporter System. No analysis of the cases is provided, but the researcher will find citing cases that are not yet in the regular Shepard's coverage. Thus, Shepard's PreView is always more current than Shepard's, though there may be some overlap. A printed publication, *Shepard's Express* (available in most states), is roughly equivalent to Shepard's PreView. See Illustration 3.

To locate all citing cases published since the coverage in Shepard's PreView (if using WESTLAW) or the coverage in Shepard's (if using LEXIS), Quick*Cite* and LEXCITE have been developed. The researcher enters a citation to a case and the computer software will formulate the search query and run the search. This is the equivalent of using the CALR system as a citator. That is, a search query is composed for the searcher which will find all other cases (in the datebases and library files you specify) citing your case.[11] Effectively then, using one of these two services updates the citing cases found in Shepard's and Shepard's PreView. Your query can be run in any database you choose. In addition, the query can be limited by date so as not to duplicate citing cases already located.

Quick*Cite* and LEXCITE will retrieve any cases in the databases being searched which cite the case you are verifying. Thus, a table similar to Shepard's is not retrieved. Instead LEXCITE and Quick*Cite* identify cases citing your case and produce a list of those case documents. The researcher can browse through the cases quickly looking for how the case is referred to in the most recent cases or print out a list of cites. Note that the Quick*Cite* and LEXCITE searches permit immediate access to the citing cases. These services have actually performed a fulltext word search of the database documents.

---

11. For example, on WESTLAW, this search was created by the system when the researcher asked the system to Quick*Cite* 480 U.S. 202:

(california /s cabazon +3 band +3 mission +3 indians) "480 U.S. 202" "107 S.Ct. 1083" & added date(aft 9/1992)

This search will look for any variation of the title of the case or the cite to the U.S. Reports or the cite to the Supreme Court Reporter and limit to cases added to the database after September 1992.

ILLUSTRATION 3

Shepard's PreView on WESTLAW
(More Current than Shepard's)

Shepard's PreView   PAGE 1

SHEPARD'S PREVIEW   PAGE 1 OF 3

Citations to: **480 U.S. 202**
California v. Cabazon Band of Mission Indians
(U.S.Cal.1987)

Retrieval
No.   ------------Citation-----------
           (107 S.Ct. 1083)   Same Text
           (94 L.Ed.2d 244)   Same Text

                  Cir. 1
   1   798 F.Supp. 94, 99

                  Cir. 5
   2   964 F.2d 1536, 1538

                  Cir. 9
   3   967 F.2d 1404, 1410
   4   967 F.2d 1404, 1411

                  Cir. 9
   1   980 F.2d 590, 595
   2   980 F.2d 590, 598
   3   788 F.Supp. 1498, 1502
   4   788 F.Supp. 1498, 1503
   5   788 F.Supp. 1498, 1504
   6   788 F.Supp. 1498, 1506
   7   788 F.Supp. 1513, 1521
   8   796 F.Supp. 1292, 1294
   9   796 F.Supp. 1292, 1295
  10   796 F.Supp. 1292, 1296
  11   796 F.Supp. 1292, 1297
  12   796 F.Supp. 1292, 1298

                  Cir. 10
  13   967 F.2d 1425, 1428

Note: Citing references are only from West Reporters. See SCOPE for a list.
         Check Shepard's (SH), Insta–Cite (IC), and Quick*Cite* (QC).
Copyright (C) 1993 Shepard's/McGraw–Hill, Inc. and West Publishing Company

ILLUSTRATION 4

The Most Current Citation Verification Services

AUTO–CITE SERVICE ON LEXIS

Auto–Cite (R) Citation Service, (c) 1993 Lawyers Cooperative Publishing

480 U.S. 202:

CITATION YOU ENTERED:

California v. Cabazon Band of Mission Indians*1, 480 U.S. 202, 94 L.Ed.2d 244, 107 S.Ct. 1083, 55 U.S.L.W. 4225 (1987)

PRIOR HISTORY:

Cabazon Band of Mission Indians v. County of Riverside, 783 F.2d 900 (9th Cir.Cal.1986)

> juris. postponed, California v. Cabazon Band of Mission Indians, 476 U.S. 1168, 90 L.Ed.2d 975, 106 S.Ct. 2888, 54 U.S.L.W. 3809 (1986)
>> mot. denied, California v. Cabazon Band of Mission Indians, 479 U.S. 927, 93 L.Ed.2d 349, 107 S.Ct. 395 (1986)
>> and mot. granted, California v. Cabazon Band of Mission Indians, 479 U.S. 1026, 93 L.Ed.2d 823, 107 S.Ct. 867 (1987)
> and aff'd, remanded, (BY CITATION YOU ENTERED)
> and (disagreed with by United States v. Hurst, 951 F.2d 1490, 1991 U.S.App. LEXIS 29193, 34 Fed.R.Evid.Serv. (Callaghan) 931 (6th Cir.Tenn.1991)
>> cert. denied, Hurst v. United States, 118 L.Ed.2d 556, 1992 U.S. LEXIS 2789, 112 S.Ct. 1952, 60 U.S.L.W. 3780 (U.S.1992))

CITATION YOU ENTERED MAKES NEGATIVE REFERENCE TO:

United States v. Farris, 624 F.2d 890 (9th Cir.Wash.1980)

United States v. Dakota, 796 F.2d 186 (6th Cir.Mich.1986)

ANNOTATIONS CITING THE CASE(S) INDICATED ABOVE WITH ASTERISK(S):

* 1 Validity, construction, and application of 18 USCS sec. 1955 prohibiting illegal gambling businesses, 21 A.L.R.Fed. 708, supp sec. 2.

To search for collateral annotations referring to the annotation(s) above, type the citation and press the TRANSMIT key.

INSTA–CITE SERVICE ON WESTLAW

Insta–Cite

INSTA–CITE

CITATION: 480 U.S. 202

Direct History

1 Cabazon Band of Mission Indians v. Riverside County, State of Cal., 783 F.2d 900 (9th Cir. (Cal.), Feb 25, 1986) (NO. 84–6635)
   Jurisdiction Postponed by
2 California v. Cabazon Band of Mission Indians, 476 U.S. 1168, 106 S.Ct. 2888, 90 L.Ed.2d 975 (U.S., Jun 09, 1986) (NO. 85–1708)
   AND Judgment Affirmed and Remanded by
=> 3 **California v. Cabazon Band of Mission Indians,** 480 U.S. 202, 107 S.Ct. 1083, 94 L.Ed.2d 244, 55 U.S.L.W. 4225 (U.S.Cal., Feb 25, 1987) (NO. 85–1708)

Secondary Sources

Corpus Juris Secundum (C.J.S.) References
    42 C.J.S. Indians Sec.54 Note 70
    42 C.J.S. Indians Sec.54 Note 84
    42 C.J.S. Indians Sec.54 Note 85
    42 C.J.S. Indians Sec.57 Note 21
    42 C.J.S. Indians Sec.57 Note 23
    42 C.J.S. Indians Sec.57 Note 24
    42 C.J.S. Indians Sec.57 Note 25
    42 C.J.S. Indians Sec.57 Note 26
    42 C.J.S. Indians Sec.161 Note 38
    42 C.J.S. Indians Sec.161 Note 39
(C) Copyright West Publishing Company 1993

    The researcher can create a citator search without using LEXCITE or Quick*Cite*. To use WESTLAW or LEXIS as a citator is not part of a service per se, but is a search technique used to retrieve citing documents. A database (WESTLAW) or library and file (LEXIS) must be selected and a query must be formulated. Thus, the exact citation to a case that was used to access Shepard's, Shepard's PreView, and Insta–Cite or Auto–Cite cannot be used to perform this citator search. Typically, a citator search would look like this (with California and Cabazon being the parties' names in the case for which you hope to find citing authorities):

    LEXIS: California pre/8 Cabazon and date aft 6/1/90
    WESTLAW: California +12 Cabazon & added date(aft 6/1/90)

Only the significant part of the parties' names should be used, and the date selected should go back to the latest coverage in Shepard's or Shepard's PreView.[12] This example introduces other techniques for query formulation that are described in more detail in section IV, *infra*.

    None of the services discussed so far provide quickly summarized information which permits the researcher to see at a glance the complete history of the case being verified as well as significant negative treatment of the case. However, Insta–Cite (on WESTLAW) and Auto–Cite (on LEXIS) can be used for this kind of one-stop shopping. A researcher may only want to know if the case has been reversed on appeal (history) or overruled by a subsequent court (treat-

---

12. Using a CALR system as a citator is also an effective way to create citators that do not exist comprehensively in printed sources and to update the annotations in an annotated code. For example, by running this search in the Washington case database, you can find all cases that cite section 478–168–070 of the *Washington Administrative Code:*

    LEXIS: 478–168–070

    WESTLAW: 478–168–070

Updating the annotations in the annotated code or statutes is likewise easy. For example, in the Washington case database, a search for cases citing Wash.Rev.Code § 4.24.010 would look like this:

    LEXIS: 4.24.010 and date aft 6/1/90

    WESTLAW: 4.24.010 & added date(aft 6/1/90)

Here our code section number is used as a search term and the date begins three months before the ending date of the Interim Annotation Service pamphlet for the Code or the last pocket part.

ment) and whether the parties' names have been spelled correctly and the correct citation was written down. For these purposes Insta–Cite and Auto–Cite are ideal. There is no printed equivalent for these services. They are current to within 2–4 days of new opinions added online. EVERY CASE CITED AS AUTHORITY IN A MEMORANDUM OR BRIEF SHOULD BE CHECKED THROUGH ONE OR THE OTHER OF THESE SERVICES.

Both Insta–Cite and Auto–Cite, in response to a specific citation, retrieve the parallel citations to the case, assist in case name and citation verification, and include direct history and significant negative precedential treatment. Auto–Cite (LEXIS) will also refer the searcher to A.L.R. annotations where the case is cited, and Insta–Cite (WESTLAW) will refer to C.J.S. sections where the case is cited. See Illustration 4.

When the only case verification tool available was Shepard's Citations as a printed product, choice of the tool for our verification of case authority was relatively easy. Simply shepardizing a case to check its authority is no longer enough. Now, with six different ways to check the authority of a case, more care must be taken in the selection of the tools to do the job.

The researcher must pay more attention to the reason for using these services and understand functionally what a particular service will provide. In order not to duplicate effort, and therefore waste time and money, the most current service that retrieves the information needed should be selected. In some cases, more than one service must be used, but in almost every situation, Insta–Cite or Auto–Cite must be used.

The legal researcher in today's environment must have a solid grasp of the functional differences between Shepard's, Shepard's PreView, LEXCITE, Quick*Cite,* Insta–Cite and Auto–Cite. Although some of the information each provides is identical, the displays vary, the number of steps involved are different and the currentness of the information is not the same.

For example, LEXCITE and Quick*Cite* do searches which are the equivalent of what Shepard's does—they both list all cases citing your case. However, the Shepard's display analyzes these citing cases (when possible) by identifying jurisdiction, headnotes referred to, and treatment codes (i.e., explained, distinguished, cited in dissenting opinion, overruled). To actually see the case which cites your cases from Shepards, you must find the volume of reports in your library or online. The online reference will take you to the exact page of the reporter online which cites your case. In the printed volumes you must locate the exact page.

If you want *only*:	Use:
— parallel citations *	— Insta–Cite or Auto–Cite
— to verify spelling of case name and verify that citation is correct	— Insta–Cite or Auto–Cite
— secondary authority citing your case	— Shepard's Citators online or in print (must Shepardize official state citation if available in state citator)
— direct history of your case (your case's path through the court system) *	— Insta–Cite or Auto–Cite
— negative treatment of your case (i.e., overruled, limited, etc.) *	— Insta–Cite or Auto–Cite
— comprehensive history and treatment of your case (all cases citing your case)	— Shepard's online or in print — Shepard's PreView — WESTLAW and LEXIS as citators — LEXCITE — Quick*Cite*
— cases citing (history and treatment) your case since last published Shepard's citator	— Shepard's PreView — WESTLAW and LEXIS as citators — Quick*Cite* — LEXCITE
— cases citing (history and treatment) your case since Shepard's PreView display	— WESTLAW system as citator — Quick*Cite*
— all cases citing your case since Auto–Cite and Insta–Cite displays	— WESTLAW and LEXIS as citators — LEXCITE — Quick*Cite*

* Although Shepard's citators will provide this information as well, Insta–Cite and Auto–Cite are preferred because they are much more current.

However, the Quick*Cite* and LEXCITE searches online are much more current, but the citing cases are not analyzed in any way. If your case is cited infrequently, the researcher may find that LEXCITE or Quick*Cite* will provide faster access to the citing cases. If comprehensive treatment of your case is not necessary, Auto–Cite and Insta–Cite are more appropriate and efficient services to use. Insta–Cite and Auto–Cite will summarize the history of your case and include negative precedential treatment. You will not need to read through all the cases found by the Quick*Cite* and LEXCITE searches in order to discover that your case has been overruled.

These are but a few examples of the choices that the legal researcher must make in verifying the authority of caselaw. Shepardizing is not enough. Many of today's law students will need to educate their employers about the complexities of case verification. When asked to shepardize a case, the student should inquire about the purpose for shepardizing (to find cases in other jurisdictions, to locate secondary authority, to determine if the case has been appealed, etc.) and be ready to suggest other services which may be more efficient in answering the question. Many lawyers practice without the aid of computer-assisted legal research systems. But often relatively cheap access to CALR is available in the area, even if the attorney does not subscribe to the system. What could be more important than having confidence that the case you are relying on is still good authority?

III. CALR SEARCH BASICS

A. OVERVIEW

CALR systems are not like books. Each word in an electronic database is stored separately from the other words surrounding it in the document. It is this indexing of each word which makes the database full text and gives the researcher such power and flexibility. When a search is conducted, the computer puts those words back together to create the document(s) you retrieve.

Effective use of WESTLAW and LEXIS requires that legal researches pay far more attention to the words contained in legal documents than we have with conventional printed research tools. This attention is required because of the flexibility and power of CALR systems themselves. No indexer has intervened. You have access to the words of the judge or legislative body exactly the way they were written. If the judge uses the phrase *Ford Pinto* in an opinion and never uses the word *car* or *automobile,* your search using *car* or *automobile* will not retrieve the case about the *Ford Pinto*.[13]

In a search for automobile accident cases, where your query uses the word *automobile,* you will retrieve the contracts case that discusses the high cost of automobiles and the immigration case discussing the registration of the automobiles by a naturalized citizen as well as cases about automobile accidents. The mere retrieval of a document containing your search term does not guarantee relevance. Without an understanding of the words that make up the documents we search as well as the software written to retrieve the documents, legal researchers using computer systems are doomed to failure. Proper recognition, at the outset, of the following problem areas can result in cost-effective and productive use of CALR tools. Other full text electronic databases may have different conventions, so be sure to check each system. Standardization is not common.[14]

---

13. Keep in mind, however, that on WESTLAW a researcher searches the synopsis and digest headnotes written by a West editor as well as the full text of the judge's opinion, thus decreasing the chance that *car* or *automobile* would not be used in this document. No LEXIS editorial enhancements are added to the documents loaded online.

14. WESTLAW has introduced a new search logic which eliminates the need to be slavish to the logic of the computer. It is called WESTLAW IS NATURAL (WIN™) and is discussed more fully in section V. However, natural language searching is available only in the case, texts and periodicals, and administrative decisions databases on WESTLAW and is not available at all on LEXIS. WESTLAW intends to make natural language searching available in all full-text, non-hierarchical (e.g. statutes) databases. Therefore, it is still important to understand how the computer parses your query and to have a good overview of computer search basics.

B. DEFINITION OF A WORD

The computers used in CALR systems are impressive machines, but they are not intelligent. They do not recognize sense or meaning. These machines recognize groups of alphabetical or numerical characters called strings. So long as a character string is preceded and followed by a space, the computer will recognize it as a "word" and dutifully search for it.

For example, these are words to a CALR system:

727	philosophy
Bakke	68–148–020
a	DES
sct	5/7/80
anti-trust	contract
judgement	recieve
84–697	discrimination

The computer does not know if the string of characters (whether letters or numbers or a combination) is a misspelled word (for example, *judgement* and *recieve* in the above list) or simple nonsense.

If there is no string stored in the computer's memory exactly like the string the researcher types into the computer terminal, the computer will inform the researcher that no such word is contained in the database the researcher is searching. Such a message is generated not because the computer recognizes nonsense, but because the computer fails to find a match between material typed by the researcher and material stored in its memory. Because the computer's selection of material is not conceptually based, completely irrelevant material can satisfy what appears to be a perfectly valid search request,[15] while a combination of seemingly whimsical terms might very rapidly locate a specific document that would require a great deal of research to locate using printed search tools or which could not be located at all in printed sources.[16]

C. NOISE STOP WORDS AND COMMON WORDS

Some words occur so frequently in our language that there is no utility in having a CALR system search for them. These words are called noise or stop words. The most obvious are the character strings "the" and "an," which occur with great frequency, while rarely convey-

---

15. In searching CALR systems for the word *automobile,* all documents including the word will be retrieved. Though you may only have wanted to locate automobile accident cases, you will also retrieve non-automobile accident cases including, for example, a case which contained the following language, "I was watching a movie about automobile safety, when the projector caught fire." This same search in conventional printed tools would be less likely to hit irrelevant cases since a human indexer in reading the projector fire case would probably not index it under the subject, "automobile."

16. "I know it when I see it," as the test for obscenity, can be located quickly in the U.S. Supreme Court database. Jacobellis v. Ohio, 378 U.S. 184, 197, 84 S.Ct. 1676, 1683, 12 L.Ed.2d 793, 803 (1964) (Justice Stewart concurring).

ing substance. In LEXIS and WESTLAW, source documents contain noise words that the computer is instructed to ignore when they are transmitted in search queries.[17]

Inexperienced searchers may try to use a noise or stop word as an individual search term. The CALR system will inform the researcher that the word cannot be searched. However, the rest of your search can be run. Stop or noise words are quite common when the researcher has included a phrase as part of the search query. "Assumption of risk," "justice of the peace," "I know it when I see it" are examples of possible search queries that contain noise or stop words. Depending on the CALR system you select, you may retrieve some irrelevant hits even with the exact phrase being used as the search query. Generally, it is a good idea to search the quotation or phrase just as it is. However, you should review your results carefully, looking for irrelevant documents.

A second category of words can be searched on CALR systems but should be avoided. Conceptually, these words are similar to noise words in that they occur so frequently that they convey little substantive import. "Tax" or "taxation" might seem to be an obvious term to use in a search related to a tax issue, but these general terms are seldom necessary. The more specific terms "depletion allowance" or "501(c)(3)" are examples of better starting points for CALR tax related research.[18] The names of Reporter series (for example, F.Supp., or P.2d) should never be used as search terms except when using a service that requires citations, such as Shepard's, Shepard's PreView, Auto-Cite, or Insta-Cite. Similarly, the full caption of a case should never be used as a search term (the word "v.," as in *Roe v. Wade,* may occur millions of times in many databases, and it adds nothing to the information that the parties in the case were Roe and Wade). The researcher is not interested in the mere fact that search terms happen to occur in source documents; instead, the researcher is interested in unique or distinctive terms that will permit the computer to distinguish relevant documents from all others.

Searches for extremely common words that are not actually noise words usually increase the cost of a research session without improving results. Therefore, reject obvious, but commonplace or general terms, in favor of more distinctive, specific terms.

D. TRUNCATION

Variant word forms pose some interesting problems for the computer researcher who is searching the full text of documents in a database. How a word might actually appear in the database must be considered.

---

17. The noise words are listed in the manuals, *Westlaw Reference Manual* 491 (5th ed. 1993), *Reference Manual for the LEXIS/NEXIS Services* APP. E-1 (1991).

18. This rule is especially true if you are using one of the CALR systems' specialized databases, like the tax libraries. However, *tax* or *taxation* can be a helpful search term if combined with unusual words or facts or run in a smaller database such as a portion of a state code or a small state administrative (non-tax) file.

For example, if a researcher is looking for cases containing the word *incorporate,* we have already learned that *incorporated, incorporation, incorporates,* and *incorporating* are not the same word to the computer. Each has more than 11 letters and none matches exactly the string of characters in the search term, *incorporate.* If a document you considered relevant used the variant forms of the word *incorporate* and never used the word *incorporate* itself, your search would not retrieve that document.

In order to avoid the need to include all variant forms of every search term in the actual query, both CALR systems use a truncation symbol and a root expander. The two symbols for expanding the number of words searched for are the exclamation point (!) and the asterisk (*). The exclamation mark substitutes for any number of additional numbers or letters that might follow the root word. The asterisk substitutes for only one additional letter or character, although you can use several asterisks in the same word. Neither the exclamation point nor the asterisk can be used at the beginning of a word. Using our "incorporate" example, we can truncate the word to *incorporat!* and the CALR systems will retrieve any document containing any of the following forms of our search term

> incorporate
>
> incorporated
>
> incorporates
>
> incorporation
>
> incorporating

If we ask the CALR system to search for *incorporat **,* we will retrieve only

> incorporate
>
> incorporates
>
> incorporated

When the computer sees the asterisks ** at the end of this root, the CALR systems will locate any word matching the root and with up to two characters after the last letter. All of the other variant forms contain too many letters—more than 12. So, any word with up to two characters more than the root, *incorporat,* will not be found by the computer.[19]

What happens if we truncate before the *a* in incorporate? Truncating as *incorpor!* will retrieve all of the forms of incorporate seen above, but will also retrieve

> incorporeal

---

19. When the asterisk is embedded in a word, such as *Anders*n,* it substitutes for only one character. Thus, *Anders*n* will retrieve *Andersen* and *Anderson.* But that character must be there. For example, *Ro*gers* will retrieve *Rodgers* but not *Rogers.*

incorporeity

leading to irrelevant documents. Truncating like this, *in!*, will lead to hosts of irrelevant hits such as

incriminate

incubus

incomplete

insane

incoherent

income

This last truncation is clearly a terrible mistake. Thousands of irrelevant documents will be retrieved. However, failure to properly truncate almost every word in a search query will regularly retrieve a smaller number of documents than are probably relevant for the search being performed. If in doubt, consult a dictionary so you can determine where to break or truncate the root word. As a general rule, include in your search as many of the characters that are common to all of the variations of the root word as you can think of. And, unless you are limiting retrieval, use the exclamation symbol to find all variations of your search term. The asterisk works in more limited circumstances. When using natural language searching on WESTLAW, a feature automatically retrieves variations of a search term including forms that are not roots, for example, *know* retrieves *knew*.

E. PLURALS

One kind of word variant must be discussed separately—word plurals. To make searching easier and to increase relevant retrieval, both systems have been programmed to recognize a singular word as the equivalent of its plural. Every word that forms its plural by adding *s* or *es* or by changing *y* to *ies* will be found when the search is merely for the singular.[20] Thus, a search for the word *city* will retrieve documents including *city* or *cities*. Here, WESTLAW and LEXIS part company, however. If you enter the plural form of the word on WESTLAW, you retrieve only the plural and not the singular. On LEXIS the plural form will retrieve both the plural *and* the singular.

Term	**WESTLAW Retrieves**	**LEXIS Retrieves**
search	search, searches	search, searches
searches	searches	search, searches

Note also that on WESTLAW you can turn off the automatic pluralizer by placing the # symbol before the singular, i.e., *# damage* will retrieve *damage* but not *damages*.

---

20. WESTLAW also retrieves some irregular plurals. For example, *woman* retrieves *women*, *man* retrieves *men*.

F. COMPOUND WORDS

Compound words are also handled somewhat differently on the two CALR systems, depending on how the vendor chose to handle the hyphen (-).

On LEXIS, the hyphen is treated as a space. Thus, *post-conviction* is the same to the computer as *post conviction*. Either of these forms will retrieve the other. However, *postconviction* as one word is not the same as *post-conviction* or *post conviction*, both of which the computer sees as two words. On LEXIS in order to retrieve all three forms, your search would have to include both *postconviction* and *post-conviction* (or you may use *post conviction* instead of *post-conviction*).

On WESTLAW, the hyphenated form of the word has been normalized. That is, a search for *post-conviction* will retrieve all three forms, *postconviction, post-conviction* and *post conviction*. However, a search using *postconviction* will retrieve only that form while *post conviction* will locate *post conviction* and *post-conviction*.

Term	WESTLAW Retrieves	LEXIS Retrieves
good-will	good-will, goodwill, and good will	good-will and good will
good will	good-will and goodwill	good-will and good will
goodwill	goodwill	goodwill

G. SYNONYMS

Conventional indexes implicitly (and sometimes explicitly) lead us to think of synonyms and related terms when doing research. When the term *lawyer* fails to yield meaningful references, most researchers automatically check under *attorney* even though the index may contain no explicit cross-reference to this term. The English language permits a great deal of semantic and syntactic variety in expressing concepts. If a court is discussing an automobile accident case, just think of the number of different words that could be used by the court:

auto

car

motor vehicle

pick-up

truck

r.v.

subcompact

compact

chevy

Searches in full-text databases are likely to yield more potentially relevant cases if synonyms are used. A good thesaurus can come in handy here; or if you are unfamiliar with the area of law and no synonyms come to mind, a good treatise, encyclopedia, A.L.R. annotation, or periodical article may help you select appropriate related words.[21] Because CALR systems ordinarily search for concepts only by seeking exact correspondence of search terms to terms in source documents, researchers must anticipate alternate means of expression as well as variant word forms such as those discussed above.

Both WESTLAW and LEXIS have addressed the problem of abbreviations. WESTLAW will retrieve spacing and punctuation variations for any abbreviation as long as the normalized form is used. For example, *e.r.i.s.a.* will retrieve *erisa, e. r. i. s. a., e.r.i.s.a.,* and *e r i s a.* On LEXIS, the researcher should check the table of equivalencies where a few common abbreviations will retrieve punctuation and spacing variations.

---

21. WIN has a built-in thesaurus available online in WESTLAW. This thesaurus cannot be used for terms and connectors searching but is available for WESTLAW natural language queries. See section V.

IV. QUERY FORMULATION: TERMS AND CONNECTORS

CALR systems would be of extremely limited utility if they permitted searches for only one character string or word at a time. Because legal concepts are often subtle, it is imperative that CALR systems be able to search for several words simultaneously, and it is also crucial that the computer be able to distinguish among various relationships between words. Each system has developed several connectors that permit the researcher both to connect various words together and to specify relationships between words.[22]

The basic connectors used in CALR systems are drawn from mathematical set theory. These connectors are OR, AND, and AND NOT. In set theory and CALR systems, these connectors have precise meanings that sometimes differ from their usage in spoken language. These meanings can be understood if you think of the source documents that satisfy a specific query as a set, that is, a collection of documents that contain the word or words of the query as a common characteristic.

A. THE *OR* CONNECTOR

The OR connector is intended to be used where synonyms and alternate expressions are needed. A source document containing any one of the terms may be relevant, regardless of the absence of the other terms. In LEXIS the OR connector is represented by typing OR; in WESTLAW, *simply by a space between words.* (Note that WESTLAW will accept an OR as well.) See section IV.G for discussion of phrase searching on WESTLAW.

Assume a researcher is interested in the question whether an attorney has ever been held liable for failure to perform adequate legal research for his/her client. The word *attorney* has several synonyms, including *lawyer*. Let's see how we would translate this into a computer search.

    LEXIS: attorney or lawyer
    WESTLAW: attorney lawyer

A representation of the operation of the OR connector can best be seen through the use of Venn diagrams. In the diagrams the circles represent all documents containing the word *attorney* (set A) and the word *lawyer* (set B). The lined areas within the circle represent

---

22. Use of natural language queries eliminates the need to use connectors. However, natural language queries are currently available only on selected WESTLAW databases. But see section V.

documents retrieved by our search. Diagram 1, Column I represents the situation where no documents in the database have both the word *attorney* and the word *lawyer* in them. Together Set A and Set B create Set C (all documents with either *attorney* or *lawyer*)—A + B = C. In Column II some documents with the word *attorney* in them (Set A) also use the word *lawyer* (Set B). Again, A + B = C.

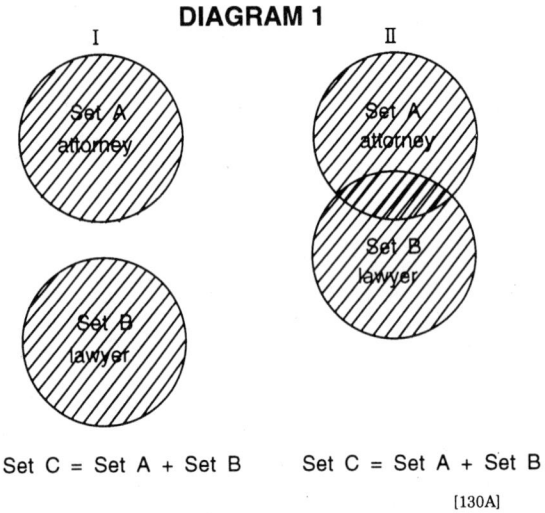

DIAGRAM 1

Set C = Set A + Set B   Set C = Set A + Set B

[130A]

The OR connector will always broaden a search and should be used primarily to connect synonyms or related concepts.

B. THE *AND* CONNECTOR

The AND connector is more restrictive than OR but is still broader than the proximity connectors that will be discussed *infra*. The AND connector requires that both words (words on either side of the AND) exist in the same document. LEXIS and WESTLAW both accept the AND or the ampersand, &, for this connector. Looking again at our research question as to whether an attorney has ever been held liable for failure to perform adequate legal research, we now look for words or phrases that must be in the same document. For relevant documents, *malpractice* and *research* should appear in the documents retrieved.

    LEXIS: malpractice and research
                  malpractice & research
    WESTLAW: malpractice & research
                  malpractice and research

Again, we can use the Venn diagram in Diagram 2 to illustrate how this works.

In Column I, no documents meet our request because Sets A and B do not overlap. No documents in the file we are searching contain both *malpractice* and *research*. However, in Column II, set C contains the

Sec. IV QUERY FORMULATION: CONNECTORS 27

documents that include both of our search terms. The AND connector, therefore, retrieves a smaller number of documents than OR but does not specify any other proximity relationship between the two words.

C. THE *AND NOT* OR *BUT NOT* CONNECTOR

The AND NOT connector (LEXIS) and % (BUT NOT) on WESTLAW can be used to exclude documents that contain certain terms. This connector should be used cautiously since excluding a term may result in the exclusion of a relevant case. For example, if you wish to locate cases containing the word *search* but not cases dealing with search and seizure, your search query would look like this:

LEXIS: search and not seizure
WESTLAW: search % seizure

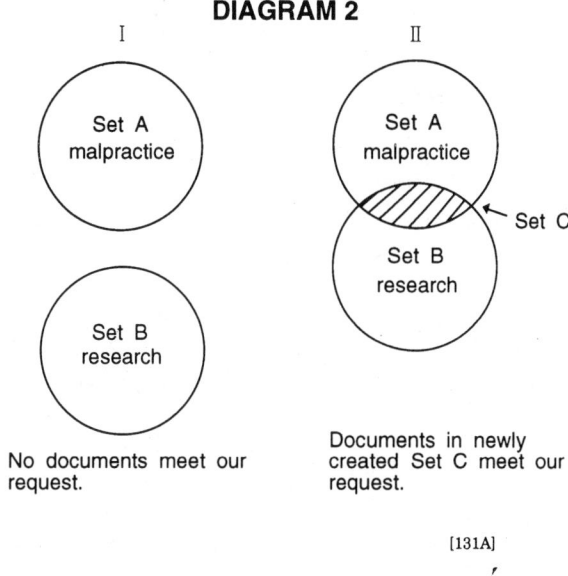

DIAGRAM 2

I — No documents meet our request.

II — Documents in newly created Set C meet our request.

[131A]

All documents containing the word to the right of the connector will be excluded from the retrieval. This connector performs the opposite of the AND connector.

The AND NOT and BUT NOT connectors should be used rarely, since with those limitations relevant documents will often be excluded. See Diagram 3.

DIAGRAM 3

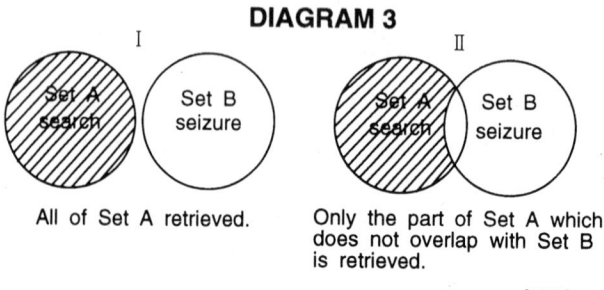

All of Set A retrieved.

Only the part of Set A which does not overlap with Set B is retrieved.

[132A]

D. MULTIPLE CONNECTORS

Both WESTLAW and LEXIS allow search statements with several terms, provided that these terms are related by connectors. For example, a search for documents discussing an attorney's failure to do adequate legal research as the basis of a malpractice action, might be represented as follows:

LEXIS: attorney or lawyer and malpractice and research
attorney & lawyer & malpractice & research

WESTLAW: attorney lawyer & malpractice & research
attorney and lawyer and malpractice and research

In Column I of Diagram 4 the set of documents represented by the shaded area is retrieved. In Column II, no documents are retrieved since there is no overlap of research with attorney or lawyer and malpractice.

DIAGRAM 4

The documents in the small shaded area are the only ones retrieved.

No documents satisfy our search.

[133A]

E. PROXIMITY CONNECTORS

Judicial opinions for a decided case may well contain two or more specified search terms satisfying the AND connector, but occurring so far from each other (for instance, one term in a concurring opinion and another in a dissenting opinion) that they do not have any real relation to each other. The computer would retrieve the case even though it is not relevant to the researcher's inquiry. To some extent retrieval of these irrelevant documents cannot be avoided in CALR systems, because the computer cannot search for ideas or concepts, but instead must locate strings of characters in specified relations that stand for ideas or concepts. Irrelevant retrievals can, however, be minimized. What is needed is a connector that allows the researcher to specify that the words occur within a certain proximity of each other.

There are two types of proximity connectors—numerical and grammatical. Numerical connectors require that the words on either side of the connector be within a specified number of words of each other. They are used when the AND connector retrieves too many irrelevant documents. Numerical connectors will narrow a search. On LEXIS, the numerical connector is expressed as W/n or /n where *n* equals any number of words from 1 to 255. WESTLAW uses the /n connector (but accepts W/n) where *n* again equals any number of words between 1 and 255.

For example, in trying to locate cases containing the phrase, *forcible entry*, the following searches would be appropriate:

LEXIS: forc! w/5 entry
                forc! /5 entry

WESTLAW: forc! /8 entry
                forc! w/8 entry

(A higher number is used for WESTLAW because that system counts every word, including stop words, whereas LEXIS does not count stop words.)

Both searches will retrieve the phrase "forcible entry," or a case in which "entry was forced," or a case which says "used force to gain entry." In all cases the word "force" or one of its variations was within 5 words of the word "entry" on LEXIS and within 8 words on WESTLAW. The numerical connector W/n or /n should be used when you are searching a phrase that may be expressed in different ways and when the ideas conveyed by your search terms are closely associated.

Both systems also permit a search for words within a certain number of each other where the word on the left must always precede the word to the right of the connector. WESTLAW expresses this concept with the + n connector (and will accept PRE/n; LEXIS with the PRE/n connector (will also accept + n). (The + connector can also be used as + s to require that the words appear in the same sentence.)

This connector is most often used when you are doing a citation field search described *infra* in section IV.H. or using the system as a citator. For example, to find cases citing *Roe v. Wade,* 410 U.S. 113 (1973), an effective search is:

    LEXIS: roe pre/5 wade
                    roe + 5 wade
    WESTLAW: roe + 5 wade
                    roe pre/5 wade

The other type of proximity connector is the grammatical connector, and it requires that search terms appear in the same grammatical unit—a sentence or paragraph. On WESTLAW the two connectors are /P and /S. /P is the most widely used connector, and it should be used if you do not know which proximity connector to select. The /S requires search terms to appear within the same sentence. For example:

    WESTLAW: discriminat! /p athlet! sport

The search will require the variant forms of *discriminate* to appear in the same paragraph as forms of *athlete* or *sport.*

    WESTLAW: proceeds /s "life insurance"

This search will retrieve documents in which the word *proceeds* is anywhere in the same sentence as the phrase *life insurance.* Use of quotation marks for a phrase is described *infra* in section IV.G.

LEXIS does not have grammatical connectors. LEXIS does have a W/SEG connector that requires the words on either side to be in the same segment or portion of the document. Depending on the size of the segment, however, this will be somewhat more restrictive than AND but is not as narrow as the WESTLAW grammatical connectors.

F. SUMMARY OF CONNECTORS

To summarize the connectors:

	LEXIS	**WESTLAW**
synonyms, alternative forms	or	no symbol (blank space between words) or
words must be in same document	and, &	& , and
to exclude words from documents	and not	% but not
within n words of each other (phrases; closely associated words)	w/n /n	/n w/n
word on left must immediately precede word on right	pre/n + n	+ n pre/n

	LEXIS	WESTLAW
words are in same paragraph	—	/p
words are in same sentence	—	/s
words are in same segment	w/seg	—
word on left must precede word on right in same sentence	—	+s

To perform research effectively online, the researcher must select the appropriate connector. Failure to do so will result in irrelevant retrievals or worse, not retrieving all relevant documents.

G. ORDER OF PROCESSING

When a number of connectors occur in a search request, the computer performs its search according to a specified hierarchy among connectors. The order in which WESTLAW and LEXIS compile connectors is arbitrary in the sense that there is no *a priori* reason why any one order is more appropriate than another. The connectors are resolved in the following order:

WESTLAW	LEXIS
space, or	or
+n, pre/n	w/n, pre/n, /n, +n
/n, w/n	w/seg
+s	not w/seg
/s	and, &
/p	and not
&, and	
%	

While the significance of this order of processing (compilation) may not seem apparent, an illustration will help clarify the issue. Assume you are looking for court opinions that include the phrase *scotch and soda* or the word *beer*. A possible search might look like this:

WESTLAW: scotch /5 soda beer
LEXIS: scotch w/5 soda or beer

Although you know what you want, that is, that you want cases with the phrase *scotch and soda* or cases containing the word *beer*, the computer will resolve the OR connector first and give you something different. Thus, in either WESTLAW or LEXIS, the CALR system will look for words on either side of the connector OR and find all cases with the word *soda* and all cases containing the word *beer*. See Column I in Diagram 5. Then the computer will join that set with all cases containing the word *scotch*. See Column II. If *scotch* is not within five words of *beer* or *soda*, the case will not be retrieved. The result—not all relevant cases will be retrieved. You do not care about the relationship between *soda* and *beer*, but the computer doesn't know that!

DIAGRAM 5

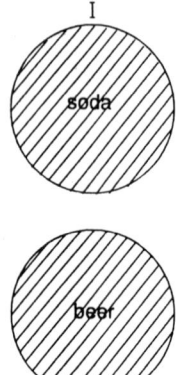
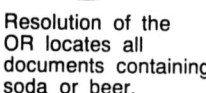
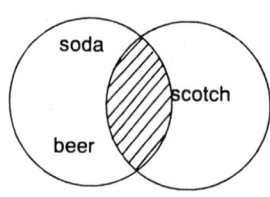

I

Resolution of the OR locates all documents containing soda or beer.

II

Combines set created in Figure I with any document containing scotch within 5 words of the set of documents created in Figure I.

[134A]

Parentheses can override the normal search order. The preceding problem can be corrected as shown in Diagram 6:

LEXIS: (scotch w/5 soda) or beer
WESTLAW: (scotch /5 soda) beer

As a practical matter, parentheses can usually help the researcher formulate his or her query so as to eliminate problems of this sort. Whenever your search request exceeds three or four words and uses a variety of connectors, the parentheses can help with the expression of the query. A poor search costs money. Plan ahead!

DIAGRAM 6

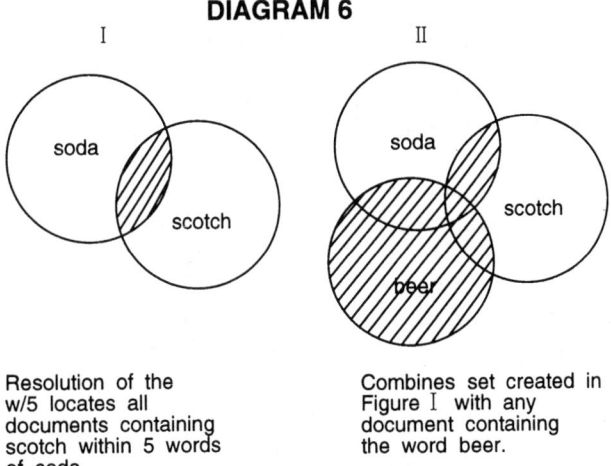

I

Resolution of the w/5 locates all documents containing scotch within 5 words of soda.

II

Combines set created in Figure I with any document containing the word beer.

[135A]

One further caution must be made at this point in using WESTLAW. Because WESTLAW assumes a space is an OR, a search for *habeas corpus* will retrieve documents containing either *habeas* or *corpus*, a result with many irrelevant hits. To search for phrases properly on WESTLAW you must enclose the phrase in quotation marks. Thus,

WESTLAW: "habeas corpus"
LEXIS: habeas corpus

Note that LEXIS uses the normal form. Because the quotation marks are easy to forget on WESTLAW, many researchers routinely type in an OR (rather than leave the space) between synonyms. Then the quotation marks are easier to remember to use for phrase searching.

H. ORGANIZATION OF DOCUMENTS IN THE DATABASES

All documents loaded into WESTLAW and LEXIS are gathered together in various groups. On WESTLAW, all documents will be found in a database or a service. Each document consists of several fields. The LEXIS system organizes their documents into libraries. Each library has one or more files and each document in the file is broken down into segments.

Thus, the two systems are organized like this:

```
         WESTLAW              LEXIS
         Database             Library
         Document             File
         Fields               Document
                                Segments
```

In order to conduct a search online, the researcher must select the database (WESTLAW) or library and file (LEXIS) in which the search will be run. This is analogous to the selection of a specific printed legal research tool, like A.L.R. annotated reports or the C.J.S. encyclopedia, in traditional legal research. Just as in traditional research, selection of the wrong computer database or file may result in poor or inaccurate results. United States district court opinions will not be found in *Federal Reporter 2d* nor will they be found in the SCT database on WESTLAW or the US file in the LEXIS GENFED library. They may be found in the DCT database on WESTLAW and in the DIST file of the GENFED library on LEXIS, information that you must obtain from a current database list or the online directory for the system you are using.

The fields (WESTLAW) and segments (LEXIS) have been created by simply dividing the source documents into parts that reflect the naturally occurring divisions in the documents themselves. This division of the documents makes CALR systems very powerful and flexible because searches can be conducted in each of the divisions. Thus, with the fields and segments of a court opinion searchable, it is possible to locate (1) a case if only the court's docket number is known, (2) cases from a specific court, (3) a case with particular party name or names, (4) a specific judge's opinions, (5) cases decided since a specific date or on Westlaw cases added to the database after a certain date, (6) cases for which some relevant words appear only in a West-created digest or synopsis, (7) dissenting opinions written by a specific judge, (8) cases assigned to a specific West digest topic, and the like. Segment and field searching substantially enhances the work that can be done on computers by making searches more efficient and faster. Segment and field searches are often most effective when combined with other search terms. Following are some examples of field and segment searches which can be run in a database of court opinions:

(1)	Docket Number	LEXIS:	number(84–1485)
		WESTLAW:	prelim(84–1485)
(2)	Limit to Court (*e.g.*, a federal court of appeals circuit)	LEXIS: WESTLAW:	court(5th or 11th) co(5 or 11)
(3)	Party Name	LEXIS:	name(boeing and microsoft)
		WESTLAW:	title(boeing & microsoft)
(4)	Judge	LEXIS:	opinionby(brennan)
		WESTLAW:	judge(brennan)
(5)	Date	LEXIS:	date aft 1980 and date bef 1989
		WESTLAW:	date(aft 1980 & bef 1989)
		LEXIS:	date is march 1993
		WESTLAW:	date(march 1993)
		WESTLAW:	added date(aft 4/1/93)
(6)	West digest	WESTLAW:	digest(common-law/8 marr!)

	or synopsis	WESTLAW:	sy("establishment clause")
(7)	Dissenting opinion	LEXIS:	dissentby(marshall)
		WESTLAW:	dissentby(marshall)
(8)	West topic	WESTLAW:	topic(Indians) or topic(209)

Note that the absence of spaces in the illustrated search requests is required form, not typographical error. Without specification of a field or segment, as in the examples, a search will be automatically conducted in the entire document, including all the segments and fields, requiring more time and yielding irrelevant documents.

Each kind of document on WESTLAW and LEXIS has different parts. The above examples illustrate some of the fields and segments in case databases. A court opinion has different parts than a section of a statutory document. See Illustrations 5–8. Refer to the most recent WESTLAW and LEXIS reference manuals for lists of fields and segments that can be searched in other types of documents. Each CALR system permits use of a single command to find out, while online, what fields or segments exist. When in a database online, LEXIS will display the segments for those documents if you press the segments key or .se. On WESTLAW, the fields will be listed in the SCOPE note for the database as well as in response to typing f while in the database.

ILLUSTRATION 5

LEXIS Segments—Court Opinion

LEVEL 1 — 1 OF 1 CASE

Name —————————[THORPE, ET UX. v. CARTE T/A Carte Real Estate Co.

Docket Number ——————————[No. 15, September Term, 1968.

Court ——————————————[Court of Appeals of Maryland

Citation ————————————[252 Md. 523; 250 A.2d 618

Date ——————————————[March 5, 1969, Decided

Action by Ross J. Carte t/a Ross J. Carte Real Estate Company against Bernard C. Thorpe and Irma F. Thorpe, his wife, for commissions alleged to be due on sale of certain real estate. From a summary judgment for plaintiff, defendants appeal.

Judgment reversed and judgment for costs entered in favor of appellants against appellee.

Appeal from the Circuit Court for Montgomery County (SHURE, J.).

The cause was argued and reargued before HAMMOND, C. J., and MARBURY, BARNES, FINAN and SINGLEY, JJ.

252 Md. 523; 250 A.2d 618

Counsel —
William C. Miller, with whom were Miller & Miller on the brief, and James Robert Miller on reargument for appellants.

Leonard C. Collins, with whom was Robert E. Bullard on the brief, for appellee.

Judge ————[HAMMOND

Opinion
HAMMOND, C.J., delivered the opinion of the Court.

Bernard C. Thorpe, a contractor, and his wife, the appellants (hereinafter collectively called Thorpe), owned a tract of land in Montgomery County which they desired to sell. Holmead, Frey and Associates had furnished Thorpe engineering and surveying services. Mr. Frey of that firm told Thorpe he thought he could find a buyer from a group he knew who "had been in it big" and Thorpe told him to "go ahead." Frey, who was unlicensed as a real estate salesman or broker, brought Eisenstadt, a licensed salesman and an employee of the appellee Ross J. Carte, a licensed broker, who trades as the Ross J. Carte Real Estate Co., to meet Thorpe. As a result, on July 21, 1965, Thorpe gave Carte an exclusive listing agreement which provided for a commission of 6% to Carte. Four days later Thorpe executed a contract to sell his property which was executed also by the purchaser and by Eisenstadt on behalf of Carte. The

[G2473]

Sec. IV   QUERY FORMULATION: CONNECTORS   37

Illustration 6

WESTLAW Fields—Court Opinion

PAGE 1

Citation — Citation   Page (P)   Database   Mode
250 A.2d 618.   FOUND DOCUMENT P 1 OF 15   MD–CS   P
(Cite as: 252 Md. 523, 250 A.2d 618)

Title —
Bernard C. THORPE et ux.
v.
Ross J. CARTE t/a Ross J. Carte Real Estate Co.
No. 15.

Prelim — Court of Appeals of Maryland.

Date — March 5, 1969.

Synopsis —
Action to recover real estate broker's commission. The Circuit Court for Montgomery County, Ralph G. Shure, J., rendered judgment for broker, and defendants appealed. The Court of Appeals, Hammond, C.J., held that where under exclusive listing agreement licensed broker was to receive commission of 6% of sales price and he orally agreed that this 6% commission was to be divided between him and finders who were not licensed brokers, and broker did not physically receive full commission and then in turn give finders a part thereof but broker orally (and later in writing) agreed that he and finders would be joint obligees under single contractual provision and that vendor rather than broker would divided commission, this contract to split commission with unlicensed finders was illegal under statutes, and broker could not recover anything on the contract.
Reversed and rendered.

COPR. (C) WEST 1993 NO CLAIM TO ORIG. U.S. GOVT. WORKS

* * *

250 A.2d 618.   FOUND DOCUMENT P 3 OF 15   MD–CS   P
(Cite as: 252 Md. 523, 250 A.2d 618)

Digest

Title — Thorpe v. Carte

[2]

Topic —
95   CONTRACTS
95I   Requisites and Validity
95I(F)   Legality of Object and of Consideration
95k135   Effect of Illegality
95k138   Relief of Parties
95k138(1) k. Enforcement of contract in general.

Court — Md. 1969.

Headnote — Generally, a party to an illegal bargain cannot recover either damages for its breach or, after rescission, performance he has rendered or its value.

COPR. (C) WEST 1993 NO CLAIM TO ORIG. U.S. GOVT. WORKS

* * *

250 A.2d 618.   FOUND DOCUMENT P 5 OF 15   MD–CS   P
(Cite as: 252 Md. 523, *524, 250 A.2d 618, **618)

*524 **618 William C. Miller, James Robert Miller, Silver Spring

Attorney — (Miller & Miller, Silver Spring, on the brief), for appellants.
**619 Leonard C. Collins, Washington, D.C. (Robert E. Bullard, Rockville, on the brief), for appellee.

Prelim — Before HAMMOND, C.J., and MARBURY, BARNES, FINAN and SINGLEY, JJ.

Judge — HAMMOND, Chief Judge.

Opinion —
Bernard C. Thorpe, a contractor, and his wife, the appellants (hereinafter collectively called Thorpe), owned a tract of land in Montgomery County which they desired to sell. Holmead, Frey and Associates had furnished Thorpe engineering and surveying services. Mr. Frey of that firm told Thorpe he thought he could find a buyer from a group he knew who 'had been in it big' and Thorpe told him to 'go ahead.' Frey, who was unlicensed as a real estate salesman or broker, brought Eisenstadt, a licensed salesman and an employee of the appellee Ross. J. Carte, a

* * *

COPR. (C) WEST 1993 NO CLAIM TO ORIG. U.S. GOVT. WORKS

38   QUERY FORMULATION: CONNECTORS   Sec. IV

ILLUSTRATION 7

LEXIS Segments—Code Document

To be able to browse preceding or succeeding code sections, transmit B. The first page of the document you are currently viewing will be displayed in FULL.

———

Heading ⎯⎯⎯ ⎡ REVISED CODE OF WASHINGTON 1988
              TITLE 18 BUSINESSES AND PROFESSIONS
              CHAPTER 18.85 REAL ESTATE BROKERS AND SALESPERSONS

Cite ⎯⎯⎯⎯⎯⎯ RCW 18.85.330 (1988)

Section ⎯ 18.85.330 Sharing commissions

Text ⎯⎯ It shall be unlawful for any licensed broker to pay any part of his commission or other compensation to any person who is not a licensed real estate broker in any state of the United States or its possessions or any province of the Dominion of Canada, or to a real estate salesman not licensed to do business for such broker; or for any licensed salesman to pay any part of his commission or other compensation to any person, whether licensed or not, except through his broker.

HISTORY: 1953 c 235 § 15; 1943 c 118 § 6; 1941 c 252 § 24; Rem. Supp. 1943 § 8340-47.

[G2475]

ILLUSTRATION 8

WESTLAW Fields—Code Document

PAGE 1

	Citation		Page (P)	Database	Mode
Citation	WA ST 18.85.330	FOUND DOCUMENT	P 1 OF 7	WA–ST–ANN	P
	West's RCWA 18.85.330				

Prelim ⎯⎯ ⎡ WEST'S REVISED CODE OF WASHINGTON ANNOTATED
              TITLE 18. BUSINESSES AND PROFESSIONS
              CHAPTER 18.85—REAL ESTATE BROKERS AND SALESPERSONS
              COPR. (c) WEST 1992 No Claim to Orig. Govt. Works

Caption ⎯ 18.85.330. Sharing commissions

Text ⎯⎯ It shall be unlawful for any licensed broker to pay any part of his commission or other compensation to any person who is not a licensed real estate broker in any state of the United States or its possessions or any province of the Dominion of Canada, or to a real estate salesman not licensed to do business for such broker; or for any licensed salesman to pay any part of his commission or other compensation to any person, whether licensed or not, except through his broker.

1989 Main Volume Credit(s)

Credit ⎯⎯ Enacted by Laws 1941, ch. 252, s 24. Amended by Laws 1943, ch. 118, s 6; Laws 1953, ch. 235, s 15.

V. QUERY FORMULATION: NATURAL LANGUAGE SEARCHING

A. OVERVIEW

WESTLAW introduced a completely new way of searching its vast databases in the Fall of 1992 with the announcement of WESTLAW IS NATURAL (WIN). This new search method is an alternative to the more traditional terms and connectors searching described in section IV of this text. It has the potential to revolutionize the use of full text computer searching. To date, LEXIS has no comparable search engine, although they are working on a competitive product.

Natural language searching is best used for concept-based inquiries. The researcher formulates a description of the research issue, which can be a question, sentence, phrase or list of concepts. WESTLAW will then retrieve the set of 20 documents that has the highest statistical probability of matching the concepts in the description entered.

Your description can be restricted by date, court, judge or attorney (like fields in terms and connectors searching). You can access the WESTLAW Thesaurus and add new concepts to your description to increase the likelihood that retrieved results will be relevant.

B. STRENGTHS

The primary advantage of natural language searching is that it is very easy to learn. A researcher does not need to think about connectors to use, in what order the query will be processed, when to truncate words, how a compound word will be read by the computer, and so on. A description of the research issue is simply formulated and transmitted to the computer. People who have been reluctant to learn to use CALR systems because of the substantial investment in time, may decide to add this legal research tool to their toolbox. However, the computer searcher must still select a database, know the commands that permit moving around in the system as well as in retrieved documents, and master viewing and printing options. But learning these functions in a relatively short period of time is very possible.

Natural language searching is more conceptually based than terms and connectors searching. Thus, issues which need conceptual expression are good candidates for natural language searching. Our ability to use the computer to help with conceptual searching cannot be underestimated. Several commentators have predicted that access to full-text databases has actually undermined the value of precedent because with only terms and connectors searching, searching for rules of law is much more difficult. Searching for cases with similar facts has been easier, however, with the result that attorneys tend to rely on cases with similar facts and not on cases which enunciate appropriate rules. Searching for concepts may minimize this trend.

Rather than display the results of your natural language search in reverse chronological order (as with terms and connectors searching), WESTLAW will produce a list of the 20 documents which most closely match your description. This list will be ranked so that the first document is the one which has the highest statistical relevance to your initial inquiry. You can ask for a larger number of documents, if you wish.

This ordering or ranking of documents can be especially helpful if the issue you are researching is governed by an important case decided years ago. Using the standard terms and connectors searching, you would retrieve this important case, but you may have to browse through many documents to find it. With natural language searching, the landmark case should be among the first few on the list.

Natural language searching should be most helpful when looking for the landmark case on a particular point of law or where the researcher wants a set of the twenty most relevant documents where there may be many cases dealing with the issue.

As with anything new, natural language searching has not been subjected to enough testing in the real world for us to know all of its advantages and disadvantages. The body of knowledge available on natural language searching will grow with our experiences.

C. LIMITATIONS

At the present time, natural language searching is available only in the case databases, the texts and periodical databases, and the administrative decisions databases on WESTLAW. It cannot yet be used in statutory databases or any of the hierarchically-arranged or abstract databases. However, WESTLAW does plan to make this search engine available for use in all of it's databases eventually. Watch documentation and online news bulletins for further information.

Natural language searching does not offer a good substitute if the online searcher is a sophisticated user of terms and connectors search logic. This person may use the system very effectively and find that natural language searching does not retrieve enough of the appropriate documents.

Another limitation of natural language searching is the consequence of one of its strengths. Since natural language searching is so easy to use, novice computer users may not realize that the question they want an answer to needs terms and connectors searching. Consequently, novice users may not even bother to learn terms and connectors searching because it takes more time and experience to master.

The fact that LEXIS has no natural language search equivalent operates as a real limitation to many of us who teach CALR, particularly in the law school setting. It is a fact that LEXIS can do some operations that WESTLAW cannot, that LEXIS is the CALR system of choice in many law firms, and that most law schools continue to teach their students about both WESTLAW and LEXIS. To teach only natural language searching (and consequently only WESTLAW) is simply not practical or realistic. Terms and connectors searching must continue to be taught (even WESTLAW does not advocate the complete replacement of terms and connectors queries by natural language searching).

D. CONCLUSIONS

Natural language searching is a powerful addition to computer-assisted legal research. Does it mean we can stop learning to do legal research the hard way, that is using terms and connectors searching? Not yet! To get the most out of the tremendous electronic databases we have access to, terms and connectors searching will still give us that additional flexibility. The list of strengths and weaknesses of natural language searching will continue to grow and change. The best advice is to learn both ways of searching to be certain that you can take advantage of the strengths of each method.

VI. CONDUCTING RESEARCH ON CALR SYSTEMS

A. GENERAL OBSERVATIONS

Research on CALR systems may seem radically different from research in conventionally printed materials. Though many features of the legal research process are the same for CALR or conventional legal research, results are achieved in quite different ways.

Perhaps the greatest single difference is that to use CALR systems effectively, you must make many choices consciously and explicitly. There is no index or thesaurus [23] in most online legal databases to guide our choice of the best search terms and synonyms to use. Often we can successfully use a conventional, printed research tool with only a vague notion of what we really want to find. Some luck and serendipity usually accompany traditional legal research. CALR systems require the researcher to create the index or search terms and then retrieve relevant and not irrelevant documents.

More can go wrong with CALR searches if deliberate, conscious thinking does not occur. Unfortunately, many legal researchers use conventional printed resources unconsciously. Poor or inefficient research is usually the result. Having a clear framework and process in mind—necessary for CALR research—will also help us improve our use of conventional research tools, and thus, the quality of our research product.

B. GOING ONLINE

Computer-assisted research may fit into any particular research strategy in several different places. Computers could be used to review secondary authority (to locate A.L.R. annotations, law review articles or treatises, for example) during the initial stage of research. Or CALR systems could be used to locate a specific statute or case where the citation is known. Computers can also be used to locate cases, statutes, and other documents by subject. Shepard's Citators or Insta–Cite and Auto–Cite can be used to verify the authority of a case. A more thorough discussion of how best to integrate manual and computer research appears in section VII *infra*.

For the discussion in this subsection let us assume that you have determined that computer research is appropriate to help locate the information you need. You have framed the issue(s) of your problem,

---

23. WESTLAW does provide a thesaurus database as part of its natural language search option, but it is not available to searchers of WESTLAW who use terms and connectors searching.

identified relevant words and phrases, selected the appropriate jurisdiction, and analyzed your own knowledge of the area of law. In addition, you have decided on an appropriate library and file (on LEXIS) or database (on WESTLAW), and you have written out your search query or description if you plan to use natural language searching. Your strategy has been planned and now it is time to go online!

Each system has a unique sign-on procedure that takes the researcher through a progression of steps. Current reference manuals for LEXIS and WESTLAW should be consulted for the exact procedure to be followed. After you enter your own personal password or identification number and your client name, you will see the database menu or directory screen, from which you must select a database (WESTLAW) or a library and file (LEXIS). At a prompt from the system, type in your search query exactly as you wrote it, proofread it, and transmit it to the computer with a transmit or enter key.

The CALR systems' response time is very fast, but it will vary somewhat depending on (1) the load on the remote computer facility (i.e., the number of other users trying to access the system at the same time), (2) the size of the database or file selected (the larger it is, the longer the search usually takes), (3) the complexity of the search query itself, and (4) the speed of the modem (i.e., speed with which searches and results are transmitted over telecommunications lines between you and the remote databases themselves).[24]

The results retrieved can be displayed in full text, in excerpts containing the search terms (called KWIC on LEXIS, term mode on WESTLAW), or in a list of citations of all documents that meet the search request. Ordinarily, results will be displayed in reverse chronological order, with the most current document displayed first.[25]

For most kinds of searches, the results of the query should be scanned for relevancy. This is easy to do in KWIC or term mode, where your search terms will be highlighted and displayed in excerpts of the document. A quick look at the first 8–10 documents will usually give you a very good idea about the validity of the search query you used.

Do not become discouraged if one or more retrieved documents do not appear to be relevant. Often irrelevant documents must be retrieved to avoid eliminating other, relevant documents. Ordinarily, documents may be quickly scanned and dismissed if not relevant. The possible validity of your search can also be measured by the number of

---

24. Most modems in use today transmit at a 2400 baud rate, and some schools even have 9600 baud modems. More and more schools use the Internet as the communications system and it's speed is usually much faster than 2400 baud transmission.

25. An exception to this general rule will occur when searches have been conducted in the larger ALLFEDS, ALLTAX, or STATES–OMNI files online. Here the researcher will get, for example, the cases arranged alphabetically by state or court with highest court first and then in reverse chronological order. Also, as discussed in section V, results retrieved with natural language searching are ranked by statistical relevancy not reverse chronological order.

documents you retrieve. If the retrieval rate is very high, say several hundred documents, you need to narrow your search by (1) selecting a smaller database or file to search in, (2) using more restrictive connectors (such as, /s instead of /p), (3) using a field search (such as looking only at the language in the synopsis or digest fields or syllabus segment), (4) using fewer alternative terms (synonyms), or (5) selecting words which are more unique.

If your retrieval rate is low—only 5 to 10 documents—or if you get no documents, you may have missed relevant documents. You should consider broadening your query by (1) using less restrictive connectors (for example, w/30 instead of pre /5 or w/5), (2) searching in a broader, larger database or file, (3) using root expanders (for example, *negligen!* instead of *negligent*), or (4) using more alternative terms or synonyms.

You may also choose to edit your query if most of the documents retrieved were irrelevant. Retrieval of many irrelevant documents and few, if any, relevant ones is a sign that the query was poorly conceived, that a CALR system will not be efficient and effective to use for the particular research problem, or that no documents exist which satisfy your query.

It is entirely appropriate to spend a reasonable time online scanning results, interpreting them, and formulating a modification of the original query. Remember, however, that a charge will be assessed for this time, even though the computer is idle. Because of this charge, researchers should act deliberately and productively. If the results are unexpected or irrelevant and if the researcher fails to see productive alternate search strategies within a short period of time, it is best to sign off and consider the next steps in a more leisurely fashion. Both systems permit saving, for a limited time, the last search, before signing off.

There are no hard and fast rules for evaluating and fine tuning search queries. Each researcher must develop the judgment required to examine the material retrieved by a search request and to assess the results. Often by scanning the material retrieved, a searcher can quickly identify the problem area: the need to add another word or two to the search query to get the right context; the need to use a segment or field to retrieve more relevant material; the need to provide alternative terms and so on. Then the search can be modified or edited as needed. Generally speaking, it is desirable for initial searches to tend towards overbreadth: CALR systems make it relatively easy to narrow subsequent searches, but it is often difficult to broaden a search without starting anew. For this reason, a CALR query should be formed like a funnel: wide at the mouth and tapering inward.

Once you have performed a search that retrieves as many relevant documents as you can locate, you will want to print the results. Both CALR systems permit printing of information displayed either screen by screen (online printing) or whole documents or parts of documents at one time (offline printing). Online printing tends to be slower since one

Sec. VI   CONDUCTING RESEARCH ON CALR SYSTEMS

page must be displayed then printed, then the next page is displayed then printed, then the next page is displayed and printed, and so on. Online printing requires an operator to be present to press the appropriate keys. Offline printing is permitted on both systems, but at an extra charge per line printed. No operator is necessary for an offline print once the proper commands have been given. Online and offline print commands may be sent either to a stand-alone printer or to a personal computer disk (commonly called downloading). Check the printing options in your institution.

Your decision about what to print and how to print it should be informed by an understanding of the pricing structure and your access to printed sources. Unless a document is not yet available in a printed source, reading an entire document online is not usually a good use of a CALR system. However, an offline print of the full text of a necessary document may be more economical than traveling to another library to see a copy.

C. SUMMARY

Computer-assisted legal research systems permit very powerful and flexible access to a wide variety of legal information. Locating documents with a known citation, verifying the authority of case law through Shepard's online, Insta–Cite or Auto–Cite, other mechanical-type searches on LEXIS and WESTLAW, and natural language searching on WESTLAW can be easily learned.

More problematic are the types of word searches that the systems have been designed to accept. WESTLAW and LEXIS are generally very easy to operate—so easy that the researcher often overestimates the value of what has been retrieved. In the euphoria of an obviously effective use of the computer, researchers may conclude that a search query has uncovered all the authority applicable to an issue. This may not be so for a number of reasons.

First, search results can only be as comprehensive as the query from which they are derived. A query may pinpoint unquestionably relevant material, yet fail to disclose equally relevant material that addresses the issues involved differently. Researchers should not discount the possibility that additional relevant material was eliminated by the search query; this possibility results directly from the computer's inability to search for ideas or concepts as opposed to words. There is also a danger that the CALR system will only reinforce the researcher's limited understanding of an area of law: while a researcher would have formulated a query to account for alternate concepts were he or she aware of them, retrieval of relevant material that fails to discuss other concepts naturally encourages the belief that such concepts do not exist.

Second, search results are limited by the coverage of the database or file searched. Obviously, the computer cannot retrieve material that has not been stored in its memory. While it does not happen often, sometimes recent decisions become available in conventional form prior to appearing on CALR systems. The circumstances under which this may occur differ for LEXIS and WESTLAW, but in both systems it is possible that recent authority exists in print format yet is not available in the CALR database. More commonly, a researcher may discover that older authority is simply not available on the CALR system. Only rarely does either WESTLAW or LEXIS purport to make available all the reported decisions of any given court. In most instances, the CALR system specifies a date and attempts to provide complete coverage thereafter. Prudent researchers will remember to search for earlier authority by conventional means unless retrieved material makes clear that such a step is unnecessary.

VII. INTEGRATING MANUAL AND COMPUTER RESEARCH [26]

A. THE NATURE OF LEGAL RESEARCH TOOLS

CALR systems, though powerful, have not and probably will not ever totally replace printed conventional legal research tools. There are many reasons for this, the most important of which is that printed tools and computerized tools are different! [27] They are arranged differently, and they give us access to different kinds of information in different ways. Though many printed products have been put into the LEXIS and WESTLAW databases, the mere computerizing of the information has not cured all the weaknesses of the printed product. But neither are CALR systems perfect and always better than the printed products. What is important is that each legal researcher must educate himself or herself conceptually about the literature of the law. Lawyers, law librarians, law students, and law professors

> ... need to know the principles of structure and design of the legal research systems. They need to know enough about the scheme of research to *evaluate the quality of the tools and the quality of the information they find in them.* As lawyers, they must be self-sufficient enough in research that they can at least evaluate their own work and the work of others ... (emphasis added).[28]

What characterizes the legal research tools we use? And how do these characteristics affect the research we perform and our intelligent selection of the best research tools to use?

Most are kept up-to-date, and all legal research tools—computerized and manual—contain numbers and letters arranged to form words, phrases and citations. Though manual and computerized tools have these two characteristics in common, the manner of access we have to them is quite different. In essence, access to printed (manual) sources is through hierarchically arranged indexes and tables of contents while

---

26. This section is substantially taken from a more comprehensive article written by Professor Hazelton entitled, "An Essay on Integrating Manual and Computer Legal Research" in *The Spirit of Law Librarianship: A Reader,* R. Mersky and R. Leiter, eds. (Rothman 1991). Copyright © Penny A. Hazelton.

27. Other reasons include (1) much of the printed legal authority is not on CALR systems and never will be because converting it to machine-readable format will simply not be economical or accurate enough; (2) it is still less expensive to subscribe to and store many printed legal research tools than it is to read documents online or to rely on CALR systems for hard copy; (3) actual access to documents in a CALR system requires hardware and a telephone line or access to the Internet—only one person can use a terminal at one time while many people can simultaneously access different volumes of, say, the *Pacific Reporter 2d.*

28. Berring and Vanden Heuvel, *Legal Research: Should Students Learn it or Wing it?,* 81 Law Libr.J. 431, 443–4 (1989).

access to computerized research tools, LEXIS and WESTLAW, is through every single word in the case or document (full-text access).[29] Actual access to the full-text documents that have been loaded into computer databases is provided not by the mere fact of their being in machine-readable form but by the concordances [30] created and the design of software used to search and retrieve the "words" in these databases. The "index" to WESTLAW or LEXIS is created first by the search software and its broad or limited capabilities and secondly, to some limited extent, by the user.

The most common kind of indexing in printed legal research tools is subject indexing. Because most researchers need access to legal literature by subject and because most research problems deal with subjects based upon more than one idea, indexes in legal literature tend to be stacked or precoordinated.[31] Indexing in the West printed system, for example, is deep—often five to six subdivisions from the initial entry.

The advantages of the index access to printed legal research tools are familiar to attorneys and librarians alike:

(1) Once a relevant general or main index term is selected in a treatise, digest, or statute, much irrelevant material is automatically eliminated.

(2) Judgment of a human—someone familiar with legal concepts and terms—is interposed between a researcher and the raw material of the case, statute, or regulation. Concepts are generally well-indexed.

The disadvantages of printed materials are also very well known:

(1) Error by the indexer could result in a lost or misplaced case, statute, or idea.

(2) Facts are usually poorly indexed.

(3) Deep index stacking or layering can cause retrieval problems. On the other hand, simple indexing under only one or two relevant terms may inhibit access.

---

29. Among the documents searchable in full-text on CALR systems (primarily WESTLAW) are indexes such as those accompanying statutes or the recently added Key Number Service. Thus, some hierarchically arranged material is found in CALR systems, but it is unlike its print equivalent in that every word of the index is searchable directly.

30. A concordance is simply a list of every word used in every document, alphabetically or numerically arranged. In CALR systems, each word is then assigned a numerical address which permits the computer to compare addresses to locate search terms required by the user.

31. Legal documents require an indexing scheme that joins several different concepts together for proper specificity. Thus, terms are stacked. For example, you might look initially under Death with a subheading Child and the third level By Wrongful Act. This indexing

Death
   Child
      By Wrongful Act

conveys a reference to a portion of the book that contains information about the death of a child by wrongful act. For an excellent discussion of indexing theory as applied to legal publications see, Dabney, *The Curse of Thamus: An Analysis of Full-Text Legal Document Retrieval,* 78 Law Libr.J. 1, 9–14 (1986).

(4) Access to printed sources is very poor if the researcher has only partial or wrong information or knows only information that traditionally is not indexed, such as a docket number, name of the attorney who handled the case, or the judge who wrote the opinion.

(5) Printing and publishing in a cost-effective manner is very time-consuming and normally results in delays.

On the other hand, the advantages of full-text databases and free-text searching turn many of the disadvantages of print sources full circle:

(1) Ideally, full-text databases with powerful search software give the researcher access to every potentially significant word in the database. Thus, fact patterns are easily retrievable.

(2) The system is flexible enough to permit a search for any combination of words, phrases, and numbers. The researcher is not limited by a rigid thesaurus or an indexer's terminology.

(3) Access with partial, wrong, or non-traditional information is usually quite good.

(4) CALR systems can be potentially more current than print sources.

Though these are powerful advantages, the following disadvantages of CALR systems, based on their full-text arrangement and searchability, are very real indeed:

(1) Noise or stop words on CALR systems are not usually searchable. So you do not *really* have access to every word.

(2) Searches that include very common words (such as court, federal, jury, defendant, supreme) normally retrieve so many documents that the searches are not very helpful.

(3) Because CALR systems are literal and search for only the words requested by the researcher, relevant documents can be missed if many alternative terms have been used in different documents to express the same fact or idea.

(4) Ambiguous words can cause irrelevant retrievals.

(5) Complex legal concepts and words in a particular context may be difficult to retrieve.[32]

(6) Searches for words that have several spellings (i.e., M'Naughten or M'Naghten Rule) or abbreviations and

---

32. See section V, *supra*, for discussion of natural language searching as it may negate this disadvantage.

words in the databases that are commonly misspelled will miss relevant cases if all variations are not used.[33]

Though the nature of the legal research tools we have to use tells us a great deal about when to use printed documents and when to use computerized research, there are several other variables to consider.

B. VARIABLES THAT WILL AFFECT SELECTION OF RESEARCH TOOLS

At times a choice must be made. The factors that will affect the researcher's choice of manual tools or computerized databases are:

1. Speed required.
2. Physical location of research tools.
3. Level of experience in use of research tools.
4. Knowledge of contents.
5. Researcher's general knowledge of the area of law.
6. Currentness of answer required.
7. Comprehensiveness of search.
8. Relative cost.

Each of these variables will be discussed. However, keep in mind that how each factor affects your choice of tools depends on your own personal research expertise, as well as on the interplay among the factors themselves.

Getting an answer quickly is always important. Though the computer systems will always perform the tasks you request quickly (if no system malfunction occurs), you may not get the result you require quickly. If you push the wrong key, forget a step, or must revise your search because it retrieved 3000 cases, that fast search may be so prolonged that faster results could have been obtained using manual tools. On the other hand, if you must research a complex issue in just a few hours, computerized tools may be needed to do the job at all in the given time period.

The physical location of the research tools you need will also affect your choice of tool. If you have a personal computer with modem in your office and all other legal materials (i.e., manual research tools) are in a library two floors away or down the hall, you are likely to use the closest source. The looseleaf set on labor in your office is easy and handy to use—as long as you are in your office.

Inexperience with any particular set of books or CALR system will certainly affect the selection of a tool. BNA's *Labor Relations Reporter* is a forbidding research tool to the inexperienced labor researcher. The novice will spend a lot more time to understand how it works and may, therefore, choose to try to find the answer using a less complicated

---

[33]. Both CALR systems have some normalized or equivalent forms that solve some of these problems. See section III G, *supra*.

resource. On the other hand, the researcher who uses this looseleaf service often is much more likely to use the set efficiently in solving a client's problem. Thus, all other things being equal, repeated use of familiar manual or computerized tools is the norm and will limit the range of choices the researcher will make.

Another important variable is the researcher's knowledge of the contents and coverage of the selected research tool. For example, you cannot locate the pertinent regulation in a state administrative code when that code has not been loaded on WESTLAW or LEXIS. You cannot, in 1993, Shepardize all state statutes or search online for Oklahoma cases prior to 1944. Even if the printed source is available online, the content of the CALR databases and libraries is not necessarily the same as the content in the printed sources of the same tool. Similarly, familiarity with the contents of printed sources is equally important. For example, U.S. district court opinions since 1932 cannot be located in the *Federal Reporter,* and CCH's *Federal Banking Law Reporter* does not include the FDIC Enforcement Decisions.

Each researcher must analyze the depth of his or her own knowledge in the area to be researched. Little knowledge of a complex area such as antitrust will make first use of computerized tools very difficult. The legal jargon in the antitrust field is highly specialized, and a novice will have a difficult time framing appropriate search queries. On the other hand, a veteran labor lawyer may well go directly to the specialized labor files online to research her problem.

Is the answer to your legal research problem one likely to be covered only in the most recent case law? Computerized tools may be the only way to find the most recent cases in fast-developing areas of law. Thus, the first cases dealing with the right of a child with the AIDS virus to attend public school might have been hard to locate in printed sources in 1990. Similarly, to get the text of a U.S. Supreme Court decision on the day it is decided—if you don't live in Washington, D.C.—you must use a CALR system. Conversely, CALR systems are likely to be of scant help if you need to know the statutory provision in effect in 1950 in Indiana regarding the validity of common law marriages.

Must your search locate every case or article on a certain point of law? Or do you just want to locate the landmark cases dealing with the right to a trial by jury? Comprehensive searches can sometimes be handled only by using a CALR system, especially if the query is not complicated and involves the appearance of a specific word or phrase in the database. On the other hand, if the search query is complex, comprehensiveness may not be the result. In my experience, locating the landmark jury trial cases via computer can be a frustrating experience. Several books about the U.S. Supreme Court and the U.S. Constitution provide faster and more accurate access to these important cases.

Actual or perceived cost of a research tool or the use of that tool will also affect the ultimate choice between a manual and computerized resource. Most lawyers who do research are unaware of the cost of most law books, but they do think in terms of the time they will take to do the research itself. The annual cost of a looseleaf service is not usually divided among only those clients whose lawyers actually use the set. It is charged to overhead—the library—and rarely billed out directly to the client. Because of the billing practices of CALR systems, the "cost" of doing research on computers is much more visible to the user. Normally, use of CALR systems is billed directly to the client. Though cost is an important variable to consider, ultimately most researchers are simply using their best (but often uninformed) guess about the relative cost of the research tool they select and the relative cost of the time they devote to research. In addition, the high start-up costs of CALR systems as well as the high price tags on sophisticated looseleaf or current awareness services reduce choice when the service (electronic or print form) is not even available to the researcher.

All eight of the variables discussed above will affect the decision-making process in your choice of a research tool or tools. They may well dictate your selection of a particular tool. Ultimately, however, the nature of the legal question, problem, or issue you must research should dictate your selection of a particular printed or computerized resource. Your selection of a research tool must be informed by an understanding of the kinds of questions and research steps that lend themselves to manual or to computerized tools. When we understand how printed and computerized tools are constructed and the structure that makes them accessible to us, we can think about the formulation of guidelines based on this knowledge.

There are no firm rules in this developing area. Generalizing is always dangerous, at best. However, guidelines can be helpful in providing some assistance to legal researchers who struggle daily with the need to find information in the most efficient possible way. Some guidelines are stated in the following subsection. Each of these guidelines can be disproved; but my experience and the experience of others suggest that these rule-of-thumb are valid more often than not. As we gain more experience with computerized systems and as these systems change and grow, the list of guidelines must also grow and develop.[34] Only when we have sufficient experience with all kinds of legal research tools can we integrate the use of these various systems to become productive researchers.

C. MANUAL RESEARCH TOOLS ARE BETTER WHEN

... too many synonyms are required to retrieve all relevant documents

---

34. For example, natural language searching is likely to modify at least one of these general rules—searching for complex concepts. See section V *supra*. In addition, the availability on WESTLAW of the Digest indexes may make CALR systems a more effective way to search for complex concepts and procedural issues.

... words are ambiguous
... complex concepts and legal theories need to be explored
... searches can only be expressed in common words
... the question is a procedural one
... mandatory authority on point cannot be located and analogous situations must be considered
... words have several spelling or form variations
... code-type materials must be consulted by subject
... you find nothing or too much (information overload).

Many words can be used to refer to the same thing. Professors Jacobstein and Mersky list the possibilities when a court discusses a ten-year-old boy:

| boy | child | youth | infant |
| minor | juvenile | ten-year-old | young man |

The court could also refer to him by using words showing his relationship to something else, including his connection to the case itself:

son	brother	ward	student
pupil	victim	witness	plaintiff
defendant	appellant	petitioner	patient

and many others too numerous to list.[35]

Computer searches that do not contain all possible synonyms are most likely to achieve incomplete results. A surprising number of death penalty cases are missed by a computer search for "death penalty" or "capital punishment". Many judges never use either of these phrases but instead say that the defendant was sentenced to die. If your search can only be formulated with the use of a word with many synonyms, selection of a manual tool for the problem may make your results more relevant and helpful. Or you must be careful to include all possible synonyms.

The opposite problem results from the use of ambiguous words—words that could have any one of several meanings depending upon context. The word *release* can be a noun that refers to the discharge of an obligation or responsibility, but it is also a verb that means to relinquish or to give up. A full-text search in a CALR system for the word *release!* will find cases in which a prisoner was released from the city jail, as well as cases in which the plaintiff had signed the release provided by the insurance carrier. *Aids* is a verb as well as a noun, and a simple search for the word *aids* in a computer database to locate recent cases involving the AIDS virus will retrieve many irrelevant

---

[35]. M. Jacobstein & R. Mersky, Fundamentals of Legal Research 432 (1987 ed.).

documents.[36] A knowledgeable searcher must anticipate the problem created by ambiguous words and modify the search to look for a word or phrase likely to put the search term in the proper context for more, relevant hits. Often this context is hard to provide, and the researcher will find manual research tools more reliable.

Doing computer searches for complex legal concepts and theories can be very difficult.[37] To use the computer, the researcher must be able to express these concepts in words and phrases. And judges often do not use exactly the same words to express the same idea. A judge can talk about a statute being overbroad without ever using the words *overbroad* or *overbreadth*. In addition, these expressions of concepts often use only common words and lead to very poor computer retrieval results. Here, the judgment of an indexer may be of great help to you, and the manual tools may well provide a more relevant response.

Searches that can be expressed only in common words can be very tricky on the computer. Consider this question:

> If a person waives his or her right to a trial by jury in one trial, can a jury trial still be demanded in a subsequent new trial of the same matter?[38]

Thousands of irrelevant cases are bound to be retrieved on the computer with any combination of these words in your search. Any words you select as search terms are simply too commonly found in legal databases.

In a related situation, a computer search is ineffective if the most relevant words are stop or noise words (those that occur so frequently in the databases that the CALR systems have been programmed not to search for them.) For example, a computer search for "as is" clauses in sales contracts will be difficult on LEXIS since both words are invisible to the computer. WESTLAW can search all words except *the* as long as the words are in a phrase or hyphenated word. Unless an unusual word can be combined with these common words or on WESTLAW the stop words are part of a phrase or hyphenated word. CALR systems are not a good source for this kind of research.

Procedural questions usually make poor computer searches unless they can be linked with an unusual search term or a specific court or a procedural rule.[39] Almost all procedural questions rely on common words to express their meaning. The printed texts and treatises for rules and procedural questions are varied and many. The indexing is often quite good and, in my experience, they are usually more efficient tools.

---

36. Irrelevant documents can be minimized by using a Topic field search on WESTLAW.

37. Natural language searching may significantly improve this disadvantage.

38. Jacobstein and Mersky, *supra* note 35, at 433.

39. The new Key Number Service on WESTLAW and the addition of complete indexing terms for each headnote may significantly improve this disadvantage.

When the legal researcher must try to identify an analogy to support her argument, computer searching is very difficult, if not impossible. Unless analogous situations can be identified in advance with appropriate words and phrases, a computer search cannot be contrived.

Searches that must rely on words with many spelling or form variations can be poor computer searches. The right-wrong test of criminal responsibility is expressed by the M'Naghten Rule. This rule has been spelled several different ways, among them, MacNaghten, McNaghten, M'Naghten, and M'Naughten. Or try to find cases that refer to the National Labor Relations Board as part of your search. The NLRB, the Board, the N.L.R.B., the N L R B, and the N. L. R. B. are just a few of the possibilities. Some abbreviations have been normalized by the database creators in order to minimize this problem, but the possibility of variant forms remains something a skilled researcher must consider. And if the word or phrase you must search for has many variations, you may be better off not using a CALR system.

Code-type resources include the *United States Code*, state statutes, *Code of Federal Regulations* and other similarly arranged sets of books. These sets of law books are typically arranged by subject in a complex, hierarchical fashion rather than chronologically like their case reporter brethren. Thus, the guidelines that apply in deciding between manual and computerized sources will be somewhat different. The legal researcher must take this difference in arrangement into account in the use of code-type printed and computerized products. Though the full text of many printed statutory materials has been added to the CALR systems, and this full text is searchable word-by-word, the arrangement of the words in the printed product has been carried forward by the computer. Most sections of statutes interrelate with other sections, but reviewing a section isolated from the rest may not disclose that relationship. The individual sections, read alone, are often deprived of their necessary context. One enhancement that both LEXIS and WESTLAW had to develop for these databases was one that would permit easy browsing of adjacent statutory sections, so context could be seen by the researcher.

But even this enhancement has not solved the problems associated with actually searching for words in statutory sources online. In the first place, the documents contain a much smaller number of words to search. This means the broader connectors—and, w/(larger than normal number)—usually produce more effective searches. Secondly, statutes are usually worded more concisely and are less redundant than court opinions. Therefore, the use of synonyms, or the use of different words to express the same concept, may be very important. Instead of broadening one's retrieval (which is likely in many-word documents, such as cases) to an unmanageable number, use of synonyms is more likely to help locate the actual relevant statute by giving more possible words in the database for the computer to retrieve. A search for the penalties for drunk driving using *drunk driv!* as your search will not locate that statute if throughout the code this concept is referred to as "driving under the influence of intoxicating liquor or a controlled substance." Sometimes this technique of using more synonyms will also retrieve too many irrelevant statutes.

What this means is that until all the printed tools' enhancements—indexes, annotations, history notes, and the like—are put online, subject searching of statutory files online may be of very limited value.[40] The more words there are added to the statutory databases for searching, the greater the possibility of retrieving the needed statute and related cases. Furthermore, the words used in the statute may have been enhanced by an indexer or the editor of the case annotations by the addition of common words and phrases, even if the phrase is not to be found anywhere in the statute itself. For example, "common law marriage" may appear in an index or case annotation even though this phrase does not appear in the relevant state code.

And last, manual researching is always a good alternative if you suffer from information overload. If your computer search results are never small enough to review or if your review of results leads you to broader searches that result in more relevant hits and lots of irrelevant ones—try manual sources. Pursuing a poor strategy online is a waste of time and money. Instead of helping us narrow our focus, computers can broaden what we retrieve to the point that we can't cope with the amount of material we have identified. Do not be reluctant to sign-off and try something different. It is amazing—sometimes those frustrating online searches are easy manual research problems.

D. COMPUTERIZED RESEARCH TOOLS ARE BETTER WHEN

- . . . an unusual search term, or phrase, or quotation can be used
- . . . the fact situation is unusual
- . . . the area of law is new and emerging
- . . . totally comprehensive searches are required
- . . . your searches involve the use of a segment or field
- . . . a strictly mechanical search can be done, such as Shepardizing, searching for a West key number, or tracking a citation
- . . . the question can be narrowly drawn
- . . . the information you have is not accessible in manual tools, such as opinions indexed by writing judge or searchable by docket number or with only partial information
- . . . the needed information is not yet published in printed form
- . . . the needed information will never be published in printed form

---

40. WESTLAW has state annotations and indexes in its statutory databases for nearly all 50 states while LEXIS has very few.

An unusual search term or phrase offers the best possible kind of search for a CALR system. Has the phrase "Christian nation" ever been used in a U.S. Supreme Court opinion? Has the word "reify" ever appeared in a Supreme Court case? In fact, the phrase "Christian nation" has appeared in 12 WESTLAW and 13 LEXIS U.S. Supreme Court documents. The word "reify" does not appear in any U.S. Supreme Court cases but variant forms such as "reified" and "reification" do appear.

Finding exact quotations is one of the most powerful capabilities of computerized research systems. Whether one is searching in a case law or code-type database, the incredible power of the CALR systems is fully realized. For example, retrieving the case in which Justice William Brennan said, "The bloom is off the Rose,"[41] is very easy. Even though subject access to statutory databases online is problematic, searching for quotations or specific language in a statute is a snap. How else could one discover how many places in the *United States Code* Congress required something to be filed "on or prior to December 30"?

However, be somewhat careful in your reliance on unusual words. An unusual word in one database may not be unusual in another. *Writ of coram nobis* is a relatively unusual phrase in the U.S. Supreme Court database but is very common in the Mississippi cases database, for example.

Because the court opinions have been loaded in full text, CALR can be very useful when an unusual fact situation needs to be located. Finding personal injury cases in which a mouse had been found in a coke (Coca–Cola) bottle is relatively straightforward. As long as the search terms can be combined in a way to create an unusual combination, the computer tools can perform this kind of search—results that usually cannot be located with manual tools (unless someone wrote an article or section in a treatise citing all of the mouse-in-a-coke-bottle cases).

If an area of law is new and emerging, chances are good the CALR tools should be used for two different reasons. First, the databases *should* be more current than printed tools. Secondly, if they are, new words and terms of art are more likely to be found more quickly than in manual resources. For example, a legal researcher is more likely to locate cases about drug testing in the workplace, comparable worth, state constitutional law, or AIDS with a computer database until such cases become so common that they have found niches and descriptive terms in the indexes and topic classifications of printed sources.

A striking example of the lag time between a new development and its appearance in printed sources is provided by the 1952 Patent Act. It created a new section 103, which stated that to be patentable, the

---

41. Engle v. Isaac, 456 U.S. 107, 141, 102 S.Ct. 1558, 1579, 71 L.Ed.2d 783, 809 (1982).

subject matter of the thing to be patented had to be "non-obvious." "Non-obvious," in the patent law context, took on a special, technical meaning. Even though the definition of "non-obvious" was often discussed by courts, the term "non-obvious" did not appear in the indexes or tables of contents of any printed patent books until 1966! Similarly, environmental law cases are not found collected in a separate West Digest topic called environment. The phrase environmental law was not in general use until the late 1960s when the National Environmental Policy Act was passed by Congress. West added protection of the environment to the pre-existing topic, Health, sometime during the publication of the General Digest that eventually became the Eighth Decennial Digest (1966–1976). These two examples illustrate why computer legal research tools are usually better sources for new areas of law and emerging trends.

Totally comprehensive searches are not always required in legal research, but when they are, a computer research system may be the only way to ensure complete coverage. This general rule of thumb must be modified by several ifs—if the search query or queries can be phrased precisely enough to retrieve every single relevant document; if the library or file that is being searched is complete; if there is no manual printed source that collects all the relevant documents. Doing a totally comprehensive subject search for particular kinds of cases using subject search terms is more difficult even on CALR systems, but a comprehensive CALR search for every case from the Washington Supreme Court assigned to Nuisance key number 21 can be done with reliance on the results.[42] A search in the printed digest will include only cases published to date, or the researcher might fail to check a regional reporter unit, an advance sheet, a pocket part, or a pamphlet supplement, thus missing relevant cases that would be found online.

Both LEXIS and WESTLAW have broken each document added to their systems into smaller parts. On WESTLAW, these are called fields, on LEXIS, segments. For examples of the various fields and segments see Illustrations 5–8, section IV H, *supra*. Both systems permit separate searching of these smaller parts. Most often, if the information you have can be located in a segment or field online, your search will be efficient and worth doing on a computer. For example, if a researcher wanted to locate a U.S. Supreme Court opinion and the only information she had was the name of one of the parties, Bakke, a search in the name segment (LEXIS) or title field (WESTLAW) for *Bakke* would limit retrieval to only those cases in which the word *Bakke* appears in this small portion of the opinion document. Since the word *Bakke* appears in the full text of many U.S. Supreme Court opinions, the segment/field search permits a faster retrieval of the desired case. Other common field or segment searches are using a date

---

42. WESTLAW's recent enhancement of the Topic field along with its new Key Number Service makes this especially true, even if the researcher has selected a key number which was recently changed. All of the older cases assigned to the previous topic and key number will be retrieved.

restriction; locating all cases with specific words in the digest or synopsis field or syllabus segment; locating a case when only the docket number is known; searching for cases by a specific judge or attorney, and locating all cases assigned to a specific West topic.

Strictly mechanical-type searches are the most reliable searches that can be done on CALR systems. See the full description of these searches in section II *supra*. You can Shepardize a case in a printed Shepard's Citator. But the process has been made so much easier on WESTLAW and LEXIS that Shepardizing manually is not very time (i.e., cost) effective. In the first place, citations found in the various pamphlet and newsprint supplements are integrated in the online systems with the citations found in the bound volume(s). Thus, you need look at only one list of citations for each case you Shepardize. No longer do you need to locate the first Shepard's volume in which your case is listed just to find the parallel cite! Shepardizing online also has some features not available in the printed product—for example, the ability to display a list of citing references limited to headnote number or treatment (j for dissenting; f for followed; o for overruled, etc.); the ability to see immediately the full text of any citing case; the actual description of the treatment, not just the appearance of a symbol representing the type of treatment.

Other examples of easy mechanical-type searches are using Insta–Cite and Auto–Cite; searching for cases assigned to a specific West key number and topic; citation-tracking where the searcher requires the CALR system to locate all documents containing a specific citation (LEXCITE, Quick*Cite* or using the CALR systems as a citator); and using the FIND, LEXSEE and LEXSTAT, described in section II B, *supra,* commands by which specific documents can be retrieved with the citation and appropriate command. All these types of searches are easy to conduct—and often give better or faster results than searches using manual tools. Undoubtedly WESTLAW and LEXIS will continue to improve the number and quality of these kinds of features. Here, the only thing that may inhibit use of CALR systems for these types of searches are the variables discussed *supra* in section VII B. For example, if the Shepard's citator you need is near your office, while the CALR system is on another floor, you probably will not Shepardize online.

Questions narrowly drawn tend to be best suited for computer searches. Conversely, a general question about a foreign corporation doing business in a particular state may be all but impossible using current CALR systems. The more focused your question for a computer search, the more likely you are to get relevant, precise results. Unless you have unusual words to use, general questions are not good for computer searches.

Computer searches are necessary if the type of information the researcher has cannot be accessed with manual tools. James Sprowl illustrates this nicely with a table in a 1981 article.[43] For example, searches for cases written by a specific judge on a particular topic, for a case when only the court and docket number are known, for cases in which a particular attorney argued, for all the cases decided on a particular day by a specific court are all possible using legal computer databases.

Researchers often remember only pieces of information, but not the right pieces of information, to locate a case in manual tools. Locating a case when you know only the court and the subject matter of the case, for example, can be impossible with manual tools but may be easily accomplished with CALR systems. One of the real strengths of LEXIS and WESTLAW is the ability of the systems to retrieve documents with information that is often not searchable at all in printed sources.

Using WESTLAW or LEXIS is also a logical choice if the needed information is not yet available in printed form. With CALR systems, you can usually read a copy of a court's opinion days or weeks before it can be located in a printed source. United States Supreme Court cases are now loaded on both LEXIS and WESTLAW on the same day they are handed down. The attorney in Washington state could read a copy of the *Herrera*[44] opinion the same day as the Washington, D.C. attorney who waited at the Court's Public Information Office for a printed copy.

Though the load deadline for U.S. Supreme Court cases is the same day they are decided, other courts' opinions receive a lower priority on the computer systems as well as in the printed publications. Nevertheless, the computer databases are almost always more current than print sources for court opinions. But many of the other non-case databases on WESTLAW and LEXIS are created from a print product. Note also that sometimes the agreement between the CALR vendor and the print publisher requires that the online system file be less or no more current than the print product. Some files or libraries are embargoed for a specific time period by this requirement. Thus, you should check the currency of the database or library you wish to use to see if it really is more current than the printed product. A not very well-advertised example of this is Shepard's Citations. Shepard's online was *never* and *is not* now more current than the current supplemental material published for the books.

On the other hand, more and more often the computer retrieval systems must be used to locate needed information that will not be published in any printed form. Insta–Cite and Auto–Cite are case verification tools that are not available in printed form. They are very current, and therefore, include information that would be nearly impossible to find otherwise.

In addition, a good many primary legal documents can be found only online with no printed source available. Best known for their

43. Sprowl, *Legal Research and the Computer: Where the Two Paths Cross*, 15 Clearinghouse Rev. 150, 153, n. 1 (1981).

44. Herrera v. Collins, 61 U.S.L.W. 4108 (1/25/93).

availability on LEXIS and WESTLAW are the so-called unpublished decisions of the federal district courts and the federal courts of appeal. If the cases are in specialized areas of law, these are sometimes printed in looseleaf services, but an estimated 28,000 "unpublished" opinions [45] per year are loaded in CALR systems and not found in *Federal Supplement, Federal Reporter 2d, Federal Rules Decisions, West's Bankruptcy Reporter,* or *West's Military Justice Reporter.* Similarly, the unpublished Comptroller General Decisions can be found on LEXIS and WESTLAW but not in any full-text printed form. They are only digested in a government publication. Many of the state corporate filings on WESTLAW and LEXIS have no published equivalent. Routinely in areas dealing with administrative law practice, the administrative actions—be they private letter rulings, news digests, circulars, orders, releases or whatever—are only selectively published in any print form. The CALR files are often more complete. When access to such documents is required, the CALR systems will normally be the research tool of choice.

E. SUMMARY

Legal researchers must know enough about how print sources have been created and how, when, and why they are used. This knowledge is essential to the effective integration of computerized and printed tools. Even though tremendous freedom and power belong to the user when working with online tools, the conceptual framework for most files and databases online relates to the print product on which they are based. It is relatively straight-forward to teach someone the mechanics of LEXIS and WESTLAW searching, but the full power of CALR systems will not be unleashed unless the user is intimately familiar with the printed counterparts of the online files.

The actual structure of print and computerized tools must be examined in order to see how they can best be used to solve legal problems. Skilled researchers will add to our ever-growing body of knowledge about the strengths and weaknesses of computerized and printed legal research sources. Only then will the true integration of legal research tools, that is, selecting and using the best possible legal resource in a cost-effective manner, really happen.

---

45. For a discussion on the use of unpublished opinions, see M. Rombauer, Legal Problem Solving 63–64 (West, 5th ed. 1991).

VIII. AN ILLUSTRATION OF APPLIED RESEARCH STRATEGIES

A. REFRESHER

During the preliminary analysis step of research, you have learned to identify the jurisdiction likely to control your research problem, to frame the issues, to think of words and phrases that might permit easy access to resources, and to analyze your knowledge of the area of law being researched. Should your knowledge be small or non-existent, often you must consult secondary sources to enhance your general understanding of that area of law. Once you have completed your preliminary analysis of the problem, you should search for appropriate statutes. If there is no applicable statute or if the statute located is ambiguous as applied to your problem, a search for mandatory case precedent is necessary. If mandatory authority cannot be located or is inconclusive, a search for persuasive precedent may be needed. Throughout, your research and analysis should be refined, double checked and verified.

This process or conceptual framework works whether manual and/or computerized resources are used to solve a legal research problem. Successful research requires planning and a research strategy. Planning is even more important now that computerized research tools are available.

Printed indexes, digests, and annotations all tend to direct a researcher into the conceptual categories that these tools have imposed on the areas of law they cover. Using these search tools, a researcher finds it both necessary and natural to follow the paths suggested by the imposed categories. In a sense, the issue being researched will be modified to conform to the indexing scheme the researcher is working with. Thus, the way in which the researcher views the issue involved will change as research progresses. Unlike conventional tools, CALR systems do not preimpose a conceptual scheme upon the material being searched.[46] The researcher must identify particular terms or significant concepts around which to structure research: CALR systems will not at the outset suggest these terms or concepts (unless the researcher is using natural language searching on WESTLAW and has consulted the online thesaurus); neither will a CALR system suggest an appropriate search query. If the researcher finds particular search terms ineffective, new terms must be consciously selected.

---

46. WESTLAW'S new Key Number Service allows an online user to research using the same conceptual scheme available in its print Digests.

It should be noted that WESTLAW can be used to take advantage of the editorial enhancements (synopsis, digest, and key numbers) of the West printed products loaded into its databases, just as LEXIS includes access to official syllabi and headnotes where provided by the publisher of printed products loaded into its databases. To the extent any of these editorial enhancements are conceptually based, use of them online may result in better quality searching and results.

The research steps discussed in Chapter 2 of Professor Rombauer's text, *Legal Problem Solving,* (5th ed.), will be used to illustrate the application of the suggested strategy in a real problem setting.

B. PRELIMINARY ANALYSIS

At the present time, only selected secondary sources are available in CALR systems: The A.L.R. annotation series (on LEXIS), some texts and treatises (Clark Boardman treatises are on WESTLAW), and selected looseleaf services, periodical articles, and periodical indexes (on both systems).[47] Thus, WESTLAW and LEXIS can be used early in the research process to enhance an understanding of a particular area of law. Normally, however, subject searching of primary legal materials online will be ineffective and an inefficient use of time if the researcher has little or no knowledge of the problem area.

It is very important that the legal researchers remember what they have come to the computer to do so they do not lose their way in the material available online. Never go online without a clear plan in mind. This plan should include the databases or files you will need to select, the exact search or query you wish to run, and a clear idea about the purpose for going online. Though flexibility is important in solving any legal research problem, lack of planning cannot be condoned in today's information environment. Inefficient searches in manual tools simply mean billing more researcher's time to the client. Inefficient CALR searches usually means billing expensive computer search costs as well as the researcher's time to the client. In selecting a database or file, please note that online, larger databases cost more to search. The smallest possible file containing the needed documents should always be preferred.

Before you can formulate a specific CALR query or manual search strategy, you must be sure your tentative analysis has been carefully done. Familiarize yourself with the area of law (review secondary sources), identify words and phrases that might be successful, identify a jurisdiction for your research, and formulate the question or questions that need to be researched. Review Section 6C for identifying key words and Section 6E for suggestions on formulating questions in Professor Rombauer's *Legal Problem Solving* (5th ed.).

Assume that we wish to find out whether a wife has a cause of action against her husband for a tort committed against her in the state

---

47. Both systems are adding more and more secondary material all the time. Check database directories online for the most current information.

of Washington. Following the strategy suggested above, our preliminary analysis would look something like this:

Jurisdiction: Washington state statutory and then case law
Issue: Can a wife sue her husband for a tort committed against her?
Words & Phrases: Husband and wife
                     Torts
                     Negligence
                     Marriage
                     Immune
                     Sue

Knowledge of Law: Very little; Check secondary sources such as texts or treatises, Restatements, legal encyclopedia, A.L.R. annotations (printed or online sources), or legal periodicals (printed or online sources).

Learn from secondary sources: At common law no right to sue; many states have changed the common law rule either by statute or court decision; doctrine commonly called interspousal tort immunity.

With your preliminary analysis completed, a search for relevant statutory authority is necessary.

C. SEARCH FOR STATUTES

This search can be done online or in printed materials. A set of printed books or an online file or database must be selected. The words and phrases identified in preliminary analysis must be reviewed and specific terms must be selected. The most relevant terms are probably "interspousal tort immunity" or "interspousal immunity." If one of these phrases cannot be located in our manual sources, we must think of alternative terms. Up to this point there is little difference between manual and computer searching. In printed sources, we might look under the major heading, "torts," and then under subheadings for "husband and wife," or "spouse," hoping to find a reference that combines all our important concepts—husband and wife relationship, immunity, and torts or negligence. However, if online searching is selected, the next decisions must be made. Should the universal character or root expander be used with any of these terms? What relationships exist between words? What connectors will result in the most relevant retrievals? Finally, field or segment searches should be considered if they might retrieve more accurate and reliable results.

These decisions, applied to our problem, would look like this:

Select a database or set of books: *Revised Code of Washington* (in print or on LEXIS or WESTLAW) or *Revised Code of Washington Annotated* (in print or on WESTLAW)

Choose search terms: Interspousal tort immunity

Think of alternative terms: Husband and wife
                              Negligence
                              Immune
                              Spouse
                              Interspousal immunity

For online search:
  Root expander or   Immun!
  Universal character: Spous!
                              Negligen!

  Connectors:
    WESTLAW: inter-spousal +5 immun!
    LEXIS: (interspousal or inter-spousal) pre/3 immun!
  Fields or Segments: Not needed for this search

Once a search is conducted in print or computer files, there are four possible outcomes. If you find a relevant statute, (1) the legislative enactment could expressly abolish the doctrine of interspousal tort immunity, or (2) the legislative enactment could appear to apply but really be ambiguous as applied to the facts of your research problem. If you do not find a relevant statute after this search, it is either (3) because there is no relevant statute to find or (4) because your manual or computer search did not disclose or find the relevant statute.

Note that statutory searching online can be very difficult. Statutes tend to use arcane and awkward language, and often do not use common words and phrases. In addition, since statutes are written in a hierarchical manner, many sections alone are ambiguous when the context provided by the other surrounding sections is not reviewed. We have a great deal more to learn about online searching of statutory documents.[48] For now, remember that statutes are not as wordy as court opinions, and a search that retrieves no relevant documents may simply be a poor search—one that does not use the right words in the right combinations.

While using the statutes in print or online, all researchers must pay attention to the scope and currentness of the statutory information found. In the printed source, pocket parts, supplemental pamphlets (if they exist), and advance legislative or session law services should

---

48. Though more experience in searching statutory documents is needed, one other trend will help in searching statutes online. The annotations, indexes, and tables of contents of printed annotated codes are being added to the CALR databases. At this time, WESTLAW has many more of these auxiliary databases than LEXIS. These editorial enhancements will help the researcher identify and locate relevant statutes online. For example, at this time, the result of running the search query given in the text on LEXIS is to find nothing; the result of running the same query on WESTLAW is to find a relevant statute, Wash.Rev.Code § 26.16.15, and the controlling case, Freehe v. Freehe, 81 Wash.2d 183, 500 P.2d 771 (1972). The reason for the different results is that LEXIS does not have the annotated Washington code available online while WESTLAW does. The search query terms are not used in the relevant Washington statute and therefore retrieved nothing in the search on LEXIS, but the search terms are used in editorial annotations in the WESTLAW annotated code—in the title of a cited periodical reference and in the case annotation for the *Freehe* case.

always be consulted. Online, the good researcher will always remember to check the currentness of the statutory database searched and update the research by checking any advance legislative services which might be online. CAUTION: Sometimes the online statutory information is not as current as the printed products. Carefully check coverage online by noting the last included legislative session. If this coverage seems out of date, check the printed sources as well. You will probably need to check the printed sources anyway to do a proper *Bluebook* citation.[49]

If you located a statute that unambiguously resolves the issue, you may not need to search for case authority. Often, however, no relevant statute is found or the statute is ambiguous as applied to your problem. In these latter situations, mandatory case authority must be sought.

D. SEARCH FOR MANDATORY CASE AUTHORITY

Again, this search can be performed in online or manual resources. We use the same basic steps in order to formulate our query.

Select a database or set of books: Washington cases (on WESTLAW or LEXIS)
West digest system (printed products or new Key Number Service)
A.L.R. (printed or on LEXIS)
C.J.S. or Am.Jur.2d (printed)
Revised Code of Washington Annotated (on WESTLAW)
Revised Code of Washington (on LEXIS or WESTLAW)

Choose search terms: Interspousal tort immunity

Think of alternative terms: Husband and wife
Negligence
Immune
Spouse

For online search:
  Root expander or
  Universal character: Immun!
    Spous!
    Negligen!

Connectors:
  LEXIS: (interspousal or inter-spousal) pre/3 immun!
  WESTLAW: inter-spousal + 5 immun!

Fields or Segments: Not needed for this search

The result of this research will either be the location of mandatory case authority[50] or the inability to find relevant mandatory authority. If mandatory authority cannot be found, or if authority found is

---

49. The Bluebook: A Uniform System of Citation (15th ed. 1991).

50. The result of your research is to find Freehe v. Freehe, 81 Wash.2d 183, 500 P.2d 771 (1972), which abolished the doctrine of interspousal immunity in personal injury actions.

inconclusive, the next step of identifying persuasive authority must be followed. In any event, your search for mandatory case authority should be brought down to date,[51] and any significant cases found should be Shepardized and verified on Insta–Cite or Auto–Cite. Quick-Cite and LEXCITE can be used to search for more recent history and treatment.

E. SEARCH FOR PERSUASIVE CASE AUTHORITY

Again the search query formulation described above is the same, but the databases or sets of books selected for use would normally include books or databases where cases from all jurisdictions are found. For example, instead of selecting the Washington case database on WESTLAW or LEXIS, a search for persuasive precedent would require the researcher to select the database containing all state cases or, if a digest is used, to select the General and Decennial Digests or the *Pacific Digest* over the *Washington Digest*. Often a researcher can limit a search for persuasive precedents by looking at the case law in one or two larger states or in states within the same region or in states with substantial experience with the relevant type of law. For example, Delaware is the state where many companies are incorporated. Delaware's courts handle many corporation law disputes, so their cases may cover corporation law issues more comprehensively than other states' courts. Your search should always be brought down to date, and the most significant cases should be Shepardized and verified on Insta–Cite or Auto–Cite.

The biggest danger at this point is in the retrieval of too much information—so many cases that there is not sufficient time to see where they fit. For this reason, searching for persuasive authority should only be done if the problem requires it. Try to narrow the world of information to search through if possible. Otherwise this search can be a very time-consuming one.

F. REFINE ISSUES AND ANALYSIS: DOUBLECHECK & VERIFY CASE AND STATUTORY AUTHORITY

This last, catch-all step of the legal research process is a very important one. Whether you have researched your problem manually or used CALR, refining issues is essential. Successful handling of this step requires thoughtful analysis and synthesis of the information located. Review of secondary sources, particularly legal periodicals, may be very valuable at this point since general trends in the law will often be noted, permitting the researcher to help predict what rule may be applied in the future. However, all the intelligent analysis in the world cannot overcome poor research where updating and verification have not been properly done. A variety of manual and computerized

---

51. If you are using printed sources, reporter volumes and advance sheets should be searched by subject or the appropriate case database online should be searched if access to CALR is possible. On-line case databases are far more current than printed sources.

resources can be used each step of the research trail, depending on what is being updated or verified. See section II B, *supra* for a more detailed discussion of updating case authority. Often updating the text of relevant statutory provisions and checking the authority of mandatory and persuasive case precedents should be done at the time these authorities are located. However, if some time has elapsed between the original research and communication of the final research result, verification of case authority on Insta–Cite or Auto–Cite should be done one last time to ensure that the most current information has been located.

G. SUMMARY

As you can see from the foregoing illustration in applied research strategies, manual and computerized research tools can be used interchangeably throughout the process. However, use of CALR systems is necessary in order to have the most current information. Since the case databases are almost always more current than their printed equivalents, all case research must be updated online using Insta–Cite or Auto–Cite and the system as a citator (LEXCITE or Quick*Cite*). Your choice of research tools should be guided by a comprehensive understanding of which research systems—printed and CALR—will work best for the problem at hand. No two problems will be researched in exactly the same way.

IX. MORE ABOUT NEW TECHNOLOGY: CD-ROM

A. IN GENERAL

CD-ROM, which stands for compact disc, read only memory, is one of the most recent developments in publishing circles. CD-ROM products are very similar to the audio compact discs now well established in the music industry except that the CD-ROM disc contains data not sound.

Imagine one 5-inch disc with up to 300,000 pages of text, or the equivalent of 60 volumes, stamped on it!

A laser beam cuts a reflective pattern on the disc to store the machine readable information. This information is read by focusing another laser beam on the disc. The reflection of that beam carries the information to an optical readhead.

Search software must be used to manipulate the data imprinted on the disc, and it is this software that permits the researcher to access the data on the disc in a number of different ways.

A user of CD-ROM products must have a personal computer with a monitor and a keyboard and one or more compact disc players. Optional, but normal equipment would also include a modem and a printer. Thus, as with online systems, special equipment is required in order to use CD-ROM products.

B. CHARACTERISTICS OF CD-ROM PRODUCTS

In thinking about CD-ROM products, it is very important to understand the characteristics of CD-ROM and how these relate to the characteristics of both books (printed sources) and computer retrieval systems such as LEXIS and WESTLAW.

Like books, once printed (or stamped on a disc), CD-ROM products are fixed. Thus, books and CD-ROM products are never current. Books are updated with pocket parts, pamphlet supplement, looseleaf pages, replacement volumes. CD-ROM publications tend to be updated with the reissuance of a new disc containing more current information. Good CD-ROM products, however, will also have an online update feature that permits the searcher to get the most recent information available. You can update law books by using WESTLAW or LEXIS, but you must set the book aside, locate a computer terminal and logon. Updating a CD-ROM product with an online search is usually easier and can be done in the comfort of the same terminal you have been using to search the CD–ROM library.

Another important characteristic of these three forms of legal information (books, CD–ROM, and CALR) has to do with the kind of access we have to the information. With powerful software, all of the words in the documents loaded online in a CALR system or in a CD–ROM product can be searched. You can locate a case with only a docket number or the name of the judge who wrote the opinion, for example. Although not all CD–ROM or online products actually permit complete manipulation of the machine-readable data, all of those words are theoretically available to you. Books must rely on tables of contents and indexes for their access and, though many are very powerful, most do not begin to approach the flexibility and breadth of CD–ROM and online systems.

CD–ROM technology, then, fits somewhere between the CALR system and the printed book. CD–ROM is fixed and can only be updated by access to an online updating service or through release of more current replacement discs (like a book). But the data on a CD–ROM disc is machine-readable and such a product is then very powerful—more like a CALR system.

But the primary advantage of CD–ROM technology is the potential savings in cost. All online databases in the legal area require the use of telecommunications to access their databases. The need for a modem or network capability that can link to offsite CALR systems has been discussed previously. CALR is expensive to use because as long as you are searching or reading, you incur costs based on the time you spend online. With a CD–ROM product, you are not online because you are not accessing a remote database. You are searching through the data on the disc itself, the disc you have in your office, in your disc player, or on your Local Area Network (LAN).

C. THE LEGAL CD–ROM MARKET TODAY

Many legal and non-legal CD–ROM products are now available. West Publishing Company was the first legal publisher to develop CD–ROM products, and they currently offer Wright and Miller (Federal Practice and Procedure), the Federal Taxation Library, the Federal Securities Library, the Bankruptcy Library, the Government Contracts Library, Military Justice Library and state jurisdictional libraries. In addition, the Bureau of National Affairs in conjunction with West Publishing Company has released the BNA Tax Management Portfolios. Other legal publishers such as Matthew–Bender and Prentice Hall have added their oars to the CD–ROM waters. Perhaps the best known CD–ROM product in legal education is Information Access Corporation's LegalTrac. LegalTrac (part of the InfoTrac system) contains the *Legal Resource Index,* an excellent index to legal periodical literature covering articles published since 1980.

Just where CD–ROM legal products will fit into law libraries and legal research is not quite clear. The software of these many products is not standardized, and at this time most attorneys do not have disc players. In addition, technology is just now developing hardware and software to permit multiple users to access the same CD-ROM library through Local Area Networks or to permit "jukebox" type storage of many discs.

CD-ROM products were really designed for single work station use. But their cost and equipment requirements are such that permitting access by multiple users, or at least minimizing the number of different computer work stations needed for each product, has become essential. CD-ROM technology is a little like telefacsimile. FAX was not popular until almost everyone had telefax equipment. Now it is hard to find a street corner without a FAX machine. Similarly, until "jukebox" hardware is developed and Local Area Networks (LANs) can easily access a variety of CD-ROM products, CD-ROM legal products will stay on the periphery of legal research. Once compact disc players are common equipment, more CD-ROM products will be created and more will be used in the day to day practice of law.

Most law schools will have the West CD-ROM Libraries because of a generous program by the vendor that includes some free equipment and one or two free disc subscriptions. A great many other law schools have LegalTrac or H.W. Wilson's WilsonDisc (containing its *Index to Legal Periodicals*) and the Martindale-Hubbell Law Directory or will be adding these and other new products to their law library collections. Watch for them and learn to use them.

In the legal profession we have been very spoiled by our extensive access to WESTLAW and LEXIS. A product that is not quite as current or fast, such as a CD-ROM product, is likely to wage an uphill battle in competition. Once that battle is won, however, CD-ROM products will take their place in the arsenal of the legal researcher.

CD-ROM is unlikely to completely replace either books or CALR systems since CD-ROM has its own unique set of characteristics. Many older legal materials (especially court reports and legal periodicals) are not now in machine readable form and could not be put onto compact discs economically. In addition, CD-ROM cannot ever be as current as an online service since it is fixed on the disc. Worse, several of the CD-ROM libraries now require the use of multiple discs. The Federal Tax Library produced by West has 10 discs full of text already and without a separate player for each disc or a "jukebox" arrangement, access becomes more and more cumbersome.

Watch for developments in this area. The CD-ROM technology could really substantially affect the practice of law. Many smaller companies are creating legal CD-ROM products. Perhaps the development here will be to put state primary legal materials, such as codes, cases, and administrative regulations on disc so the volume of data can actually fit onto 1 or 2 discs. State law products for Washington, New York, Illinois and New Mexico are available now. Many others are in the development stages.

X. NON-LEGAL DATABASES

In the last decade of the twentieth century, the law has become even more interwoven with the fabric of our daily lives. A good practicing attorney is likely to need non-legal as well as legal information as a matter of course. Though law students are not typically trained in law school to research non-legal questions, a good lawyer will realize the value of a wide variety of sources that may help answer factual or non-legal questions which arise in the course of the practice of law.[52]

A. NEXIS

Probably the non-legal database with which you will become most familiar is NEXIS. NEXIS is a product of Mead Data Corporation (MDC), the vendor that supplies us with LEXIS. NEXIS contains the full-text documents of hundreds of magazines, newspapers, newsletters, and wire services, including the *New York Times,* the *National Law Journal,* and the *Legal Times.* The search protocol and organization of the files is very similar to LEXIS so it is a relatively friendly database for lawyers and law students to use. In 1990, MDC began to make a substantial portion of NEXIS available to law schools under the educational contract, so NEXIS is probably a system you will be able to use while in law school.

NEXIS is particularly helpful to answer factual questions, to follow up on very current news and articles that may affect a client's case, to learn about a potential client or opposing counsel, or to read discussions about the most recent cases decided by various courts. In addition, newly developing areas of law can be tracked much easier with access to databases like NEXIS.

B. DIALOG

DIALOG is a vendor that offers access to several hundred individual databases produced by a wide variety of publishers. Excellent databases in medicine, chemistry, the environment, business, engineering, and the social sciences are included. Primarily, these databases on DIALOG are indexes and abstracting services, so a researcher is still likely to have to locate the actual document or article. In early 1991 WESTLAW began to make DIALOG available using WESTLAW protocol. About 90% of the DIALOG databases are now available on WESTLAW. These DIALOG databases are also available on the law

---

52. The best "short" overview of the non-legal research sources of value to an attorney can be found in Cohen, Berring & Olson, How to Find The Law, ch. 14 (9th ed. 1989).

school educational contracts so you should have an opportunity to use them in law school.

C. OTHERS

Several other non-legal databases are used extensively throughout the country in law firms, courts, and academic law libraries. They are listed here to acquaint you with their existence. Since searching on these systems may be complicated and expensive, discuss your research needs with your law librarian. Some law schools will perform searches for faculty and students, while other law schools do not provide access to these additional databases for students. WILSONLINE is the online version of the many indexes published by H.W. Wilson, including the important *Index to Legal Periodicals*. VU/TEXT includes the full text of over two dozen newspapers throughout the country in its database. Another database commonly used for other full-text newspaper coverage is Data-times.

Several databases track federal congressional legislation. The most commonly used database is LEGI–SLATE. Bill tracking (checking the status of a bill) is very current and is easily handled with this system. It should also be noted that many states have online databases that track pending state legislation and may include the current statutes and/or regulations. Check with your state legislative office for system availability.

All of the databases discussed above can help answer factual, legal, and non-legal questions. Ask your librarian what is available in your environment.

†